MYSTERY OF THE MERKABA

Riding the Light Chariot

D.R. T STEPHENS

S.D.N Publishing

Copyright © 2023 S.D.N Publishing

All rights reserved

The characters and events portrayed in this book are fictitious. Any similarity to real persons, living or dead, is coincidental and not intended by the author.

No part of this book may be reproduced, or stored in a retrieval system, or transmitted in any form or by any means, electronic, mechanical, photocopying, recording, or otherwise, without express written permission of the publisher.

ISBN: 9798860597402

CONTENTS

Title Page
Copyright
General Disclaimer — 1
Chapter 1: Introduction to Merkaba Mysticism — 3
Chapter 2: Geometry of the Soul — 6
Chapter 3: Ancient Origins — 9
Chapter 4: The Merkaba in the Kabbalistic Tradition — 12
Chapter 5: Eastern Connections — 15
Chapter 6: Sacred Geometry and Spirituality — 18
Chapter 7: The Metaphysical Aspect — 22
Chapter 8: Physical Manifestation of Merkaba Energy — 26
Chapter 9: Visualization Techniques — 29
Chapter 10: Advanced Visualization — 33
Chapter 11: Breathing and Meditation — 36
Chapter 12: Riding the Light Chariot: Personal Experiences — 40
Chapter 13: Dangers and Misunderstandings — 43
Chapter 14: The 17-Breath Technique — 46
Chapter 15: Merkaba and Healing — 50
Chapter 16: The Science Behind the Mysticism — 53
Chapter 17: The Merkaba and Quantum Physics — 56
Chapter 18: Building a Merkaba: Physical Models — 59

Chapter 19: Merkaba and Music	62
Chapter 20: Crystals and the Merkaba	65
Chapter 21: The Digital Age of Merkaba	68
Chapter 22: The Collective Merkaba	72
Chapter 23: Navigating Realms	75
Chapter 24: Merkaba and Dreams	78
Chapter 25: Merkaba in Popular Culture	81
Chapter 26: Debunking Myths	84
Chapter 27: Merkaba and Astrology	87
Chapter 28: Planetary Merkabas	91
Chapter 29: Teaching and Learning the Merkaba	94
Chapter 30: Ethical Considerations	98
Chapter 31: Beyond the Fifth Dimension	101
Chapter 32: Future of Merkaba Practices	105
Chapter 33: Resource Guide	108
Chapter 34: Glossary	112
Chapter 35: Frequently Asked Questions	116
Chapter 36: Conclusion and Final Thoughts	120
THE END	123

GENERAL DISCLAIMER

This book is intended to provide general information to the reader on the topics covered. The author and publisher have made every effort to ensure that the information herein is accurate and up-to-date at the time of publication. However, they do not warrant or guarantee the accuracy, completeness, adequacy, or currency of the information contained in this book. The author and publisher expressly disclaim any liability or responsibility for any errors or omissions in the content herein.

The information, guidance, advice, tips, and suggestions provided in this book are not intended to replace professional advice or consultation. Readers are strongly encouraged to consult with an appropriate professional for specific advice tailored to their situation before making any decisions or taking any actions based on the content of this book.

The views and opinions expressed in this book are those of the author and do not necessarily reflect the official policy or position of any other agency, organization, employer or company.

The author and publisher are not responsible for any actions taken or not taken by the reader based on the information, advice, or suggestions provided in this book. The reader is solely responsible for their actions and the consequences thereof.

This book is not intended to be a source of legal, business, medical or psychological advice, and readers are cautioned to seek the services of a competent professional in these or other areas of expertise.

All product names, logos, and brands are property of their respective owners. All company, product and service names used in this book are for identification purposes only. Use of these names, logos, and brands does not imply endorsement.

Readers of this book are advised to do their own due diligence when it comes to making decisions and all information, products, services and advice that have been provided should be independently verified by your own qualified professionals.

By reading this book, you agree that the author and publisher are not responsible for your success or failure resulting from any information presented in this book.

CHAPTER 1: INTRODUCTION TO MERKABA MYSTICISM

Welcome to the world of Merkaba Mysticism, a subject that has both enchanted and puzzled seekers of spiritual wisdom and understanding for centuries. In this first chapter of this extensive journey, we will discuss the fundamental characteristics of the Merkaba, including its idea, its historical beginnings, and the significance it holds in various spiritual traditions. This age-old concept serves as a meeting point for geometry, spirituality, and sometimes, even modern science. So, let's commence our exploration of the Merkaba, the mystical 'chariot' often associated with complex geometric shapes that symbolize much more than meets the eye.

The Basic Concept of Merkaba

The term "Merkaba" is of ancient origin, derived from three separate words: Mer, Ka, and Ba. In ancient Egyptian, 'Mer' refers to a specific kind of light that was understood to rotate within itself, 'Ka' alludes to the individual spirit, and 'Ba' represents the human body or reality. When combined, Merkaba essentially signifies the 'chariot' or the 'vehicle' of light that transports the spirit and the body. Though its most immediate connotations trace back to Egyptian civilization, the concept permeates through various cultures and spiritual doctrines, each interpreting it in their unique ways.

Historical Context

The Merkaba finds its presence across multiple epochs and civilizations. From the pyramids of Egypt to the texts of Jewish mysticism, and from Islamic Sufism to certain schools of Hinduism, Merkaba has been viewed, studied, and revered in many contexts. However, what remains common is its depiction as a complex geometric figure, often a three-dimensional shape made up of two equally sized, interlocked tetrahedra. This shape is believed to exist around the human body and can be activated through specific meditative and breathing techniques.

Significance in Spiritual Practices

The role of Merkaba in spiritual practices is profound and varied. In Jewish Kabbalistic traditions, it is regarded to be the heavenly light vehicle that ascended masters use to connect with higher worlds. In Eastern philosophies, Merkaba is often associated with chakra systems and is believed to offer an advanced state of meditation and cosmic travel. The concept also shows remarkable similarities with the Platonic solids in Greek philosophy, suggesting universality that crosses cultural boundaries.

Bridging Spirituality and Geometry

One of the captivating facets of the Merkaba is its geometric form, often related to the realm of 'sacred geometry.' Sacred geometry postulates that specific shapes have metaphysical and spiritual significance. In the case of Merkaba, its star-tetrahedron shape is said to represent the innermost law of the physical world: the inseparable relationship between the two complementary halves

—the positive and negative, the manifest and the unmanifest— which form a perfect equilibrium. In simpler terms, the geometric shape of the Merkaba symbolizes unity, balance, and harmony, offering a visually representable link between our corporeal existence and higher spiritual reality.

The Journey Ahead

The Merkaba is more than just a concept; it is a gateway to understanding the complex interplay between the human experience and the realms of higher consciousness. With its multifaceted nature, Merkaba serves as an intersection of history, spirituality, metaphysics, and even emerging theories in quantum physics. As we proceed through the chapters of this book, we will delve into its geometric intricacies, its manifestations in various cultures, and its potential implications for personal spiritual practices.

To summarize, the Merkaba is a symbol that has captivated the human imagination across cultures and spiritual traditions. Its rich history and profound spiritual connotations make it a fascinating subject of study, whether you're a spiritual seeker, a student of comparative religion, or even someone with a passing interest in metaphysics and sacred geometry. This introductory chapter serves as the launching pad for our deeper dive into the Mystery of the Merkaba: Riding the Light Chariot.

CHAPTER 2: GEOMETRY OF THE SOUL

In our exploration of the multifaceted concept of Merkaba, understanding its geometric basis is instrumental. Geometry, often perceived as mere mathematical abstraction, finds a rich and meaningful application in the realm of spirituality through the Merkaba. Here, we delve into the tetrahedral structure of the Merkaba and the significance of its mathematical properties in relation to the human soul.

The Tetrahedral Structure

The word Merkaba is most commonly associated with a three-dimensional, star-tetrahedral structure. In its most basic form, a star tetrahedron is composed of two interlocking tetrahedrons, with one tetrahedron facing upward and the other pointing below. One tetrahedron is a polyhedron with four faces, and each of those faces is a triangle with equilateral sides.

When you interlock two tetrahedrons, it creates a balance; this symmetry is deeply meaningful. The upward-pointing tetrahedron is often associated with masculine energy, often referred to as the "blade," while the downward-pointing tetrahedron represents feminine energy, or the "chalice." The union of the two provides a holistic representation of life energy.

Mathematical Properties

The geometry of the Merkaba is not arbitrary; rather, it has unique mathematical properties. For instance, the ratio of the edge length of the star tetrahedron to its circumscribed sphere has intriguing geometric and numerical significance. This ratio mirrors principles found in other geometric shapes like the Golden Ratio, which is ubiquitous throughout nature, art, and architecture. Mathematical constants such as Pi (π) and Phi (Φ) also manifest in the geometry, signifying that the Merkaba is tied into the fundamental structures of the universe.

Moreover, it's worth noting that the simple structure of a tetrahedron, the building block of the Merkaba, is the simplest three-dimensional shape that can exist in Euclidean space. In a way, this represents the minimalistic yet complex essence of our soul and life energy.

Symbolic Resonance

Geometry is a language, and the Merkaba speaks volumes through its form. The balance and symmetry inherent in its structure could be seen as metaphors for cosmic balance and the dualistic nature of existence: mind and body, earth and sky, physical and spiritual. In various spiritual traditions, shapes are more than just visual or tactile forms; they are reflections of underlying cosmic principles.

Merkaba and the Platonic Solids

It's interesting to note that the tetrahedron is one of the five Platonic solids, named after the ancient Greek philosopher

Plato. Platonic solids have faces, edges, and angles that are all congruent, and they are often associated with the classical elements: earth, water, air, fire, and ether. The tetrahedron, in this classification, typically represents fire, symbolizing transformation, purification, and ascendance. The Merkaba, therefore, also taps into this ancient wisdom, again reinforcing its deep-rooted connection to spirituality and the cosmos.

Multidimensional Interpretations

While we often perceive the Merkaba as a three-dimensional shape, spiritual practitioners argue that this is a limited understanding. Some propose that it extends into multiple dimensions, serving as a vehicle for inter-dimensional travel. Although this idea veers into the realm of metaphysics, it nonetheless offers an expanded view of the Merkaba, elevating it from a mere shape to a dynamic, multi-dimensional entity.

In summary, the geometry of the Merkaba serves as a potent metaphor and tool for understanding intricate spiritual concepts. Its tetrahedral form, balanced structure, and mathematical properties resonate deeply with ancient wisdom, current spiritual practices, and even the fundamental architecture of the universe. While it starts as a geometric figure, its dimensions grow in spiritual interpretations, suggesting that the Merkaba could indeed be the "geometry of the soul," an ever-expanding form encapsulating life, energy, and perhaps even the secrets of the universe.

CHAPTER 3: ANCIENT ORIGINS

In the tapestry of human spiritual and philosophical thought, the concept of the Merkaba holds a notable thread that weaves through time and culture. Having explored its geometrical aspects in the previous chapter, we now turn our attention to the historical roots of Merkaba, particularly tracing its presence in ancient civilizations such as Egypt and Mesopotamia. This journey through history not only enhances our understanding of its spiritual dimensions but also serves to illuminate how the Merkaba concept has been influenced and shaped by various cultural contexts.

The Egyptian Connection: Mer-Ka-Ba

The term Merkaba is most directly connected to the ancient Egyptian words "Mer," "Ka," and "Ba," which loosely translate to light, spirit, and body respectively. In ancient Egyptian cosmology, the "Ka" represents the individual's life-force or spiritual essence, while the "Ba" denotes the soul's physical manifestation. The "Mer" serves as a revolving field of light that envelops these two aspects, essentially describing a chariot of light that enables spiritual travel.

The concept has been interpreted in the context of Egyptian funerary texts like the "Book of the Dead," wherein the journey of the soul after death is elaborated. In these texts, the Merkaba serves as a vehicle that helps the soul traverse various celestial realms. This idea can also be linked to the Pyramids, those monumental achievements of ancient architecture. Some theories suggest that the shape and orientation of the Pyramids were designed to align with cosmic events and to facilitate the pharaoh's spiritual journey, possibly utilizing the Merkaba as a celestial chariot.

Mesopotamian Threads: The Divine Chariots

Another fertile ground where the concept of a light chariot is found is ancient Mesopotamia, among the Sumerians, Babylonians, and Assyrians. In their religious texts and iconography, there are mentions of divine chariots or vehicles often related to gods and celestial beings. Although the term "Merkaba" is not explicitly used, the concept bears striking similarities.

For instance, the Sumerian Epic of Gilgamesh, one of the earliest pieces of literature, mentions divine beings coming down from the heavens in flying chariots. The chariots in these texts are often described as emitting bright light and are typically associated with spiritual ascension or enlightenment, similar to the roles attributed to the Merkaba in other traditions.

Shared Characteristics: A Cultural Confluence

It's fascinating to observe that both Egyptian and Mesopotamian cultures share several characteristics in their understanding of the Merkaba-like concepts, despite the geographical and temporal distances. Both civilizations attributed the vehicle's function to spiritual travel or ascension and depicted it as being associated with celestial or divine entities.

However, it is essential to understand that these are not carbon copies but interpretations shaped by their respective cultures. While the Egyptians focused more on the soul's journey after death, Mesopotamians were more concerned with the interactions between gods and humans.

Academic Perspectives

The historical roots of Merkaba in these ancient civilizations have been the subject of various academic studies, ranging from comparative religion to archaeoastronomy. While some scholars caution against drawing too direct a line between these ancient practices and modern Merkaba mysticism, there is a consensus that the concept has deep historical roots that tap into a universal human fascination with the intersection of the spiritual and the celestial.

Summary

Tracing the concept of Merkaba through the ancient landscapes of Egypt and Mesopotamia opens a vista into its rich, complex origins. The idea that a vehicle made of geometric light can guide the human soul has transcended the ages, adapting to different cultural contexts yet retaining its core essence. Whether serving as a celestial chariot in Egyptian cosmology or a divine vehicle in Mesopotamian epic tales, the Merkaba has remained a compelling facet of human spirituality. It symbolizes our age-old desire to connect with the divine, to understand our place in the cosmos, and to transcend the limitations of our physical existence.

CHAPTER 4: THE MERKABA IN THE KABBALISTIC TRADITION

The Merkaba's presence is deeply felt in the Kabbalistic tradition, a form of Jewish mysticism that dates back to medieval Europe but has roots in earlier Jewish thought. Given the Merkaba's rich history, it's essential to examine how Kabbalah incorporates this geometric figure into its complex systems of thought, focusing particularly on its symbolism and position within the Tree of Life.

Symbolism in the Kabbalistic Tradition

The word 'Merkaba' can be broken down into its Hebrew components: 'Mer' meaning light, 'Ka' referring to the spirit, and 'Ba' indicating the body. In Kabbalah, the Merkaba is often seen as a vehicle of divine light that facilitates the process of spiritual ascension. This is consistent with the broader Kabbalistic themes of divine emanation and the ultimate return to the source, often represented by Ein Sof, the endless, boundless aspect of God.

Beyond mere linguistic connections, the Merkaba serves as a symbolic structure encapsulating the interplay between the physical and metaphysical realms. The lower tetrahedron represents Asiyah, the World of Action, which aligns with the physical, manifest universe. The upper tetrahedron corresponds to Atziluth, the World of Emanation, which is the pure, divine realm of God's ineffable qualities. In this configuration, the Merkaba becomes a microcosmic model of macrocosmic reality.

The Merkaba and the Tree of Life

In Kabbalistic tradition, the Tree of Life (Etz Chaim in Hebrew) is a central symbol used to understand the nature of God and the universe. It consists of ten spheres (sephiroth) connected by 22 paths. These sephiroth represent various divine attributes, and the paths signify the relationships between these attributes.

The Merkaba finds its place in the Tree of Life by aligning its geometry with the sephiroth. If you visualize the Tree, the two tetrahedrons of the Merkaba can be superimposed upon it, representing dual aspects of existence—Asiyah and Atziluth, as mentioned earlier. This alignment suggests that understanding the Merkaba could potentially grant insights into the intricate web of divine attributes and their interactions within the Tree of Life.

Practical Implications in Kabbalistic Practices

Practically, the Merkaba has been invoked in Kabbalistic meditation and rituals. For instance, some practices involve visualizing the Merkaba as a two-dimensional Star of David, which is another symbol deeply rooted in Jewish mysticism. As in other spiritual traditions, the primary purpose of these exercises is to facilitate personal transformation and divine communion.

The Merkaba also shows up in literature associated with Kabbalah. The foundational text, the Zohar, occasionally refers to the Merkaba but typically in a veiled, symbolic language. This reflects the guarded attitude traditional Kabbalists maintain towards divulging mystical secrets, emphasizing the notion that these truths are best approached through personal experience and inner revelation.

Commonality and Distinction from Other Traditions

While the essence of the Merkaba remains consistent across spiritual traditions, Kabbalah offers a uniquely Jewish lens through which to understand this geometric chariot. The Merkaba in Kabbalah is intimately tied to monotheistic beliefs and rooted in a particular cultural and historical context that shapes its interpretation. Unlike the Merkaba in some other traditions, the Kabbalistic Merkaba is not just a tool for individual spiritual ascent but also a symbol deeply connected to collective Jewish identity and destiny.

In summary, the Merkaba holds a cherished place in the heart of Kabbalistic symbolism and practice. It acts as a bridge between the divine and earthly realms, capturing the essence of what Kabbalists consider the ultimate spiritual journey. From its role in symbology to its alignment with the Tree of Life and practical usage in meditation and ritual, the Merkaba in Kabbalistic tradition offers a profound and intricate perspective on this ancient geometric figure.

CHAPTER 5: EASTERN CONNECTIONS

The term Merkaba has its roots deeply embedded in the Jewish Kabbalistic tradition and ancient civilizations like Egypt and Mesopotamia. While these origins provide an extensive basis for understanding the concept, it is equally fascinating to explore how the Merkaba resonates with Eastern philosophies. This chapter delves into the similarities and differences between the Merkaba and concepts in Eastern traditions like chakras, kundalini, and mandalas, offering a broader perspective on this intriguing geometrical form.

Merkaba and Chakras

Chakras are energy centers located at various points along the spinal column, according to Eastern philosophies, particularly in Hinduism and Buddhism. These centers are essential for the circulation of prana, or life force, much in the same way that the Merkaba is considered a vehicle for divine light and energy. When it comes to the Merkaba, it's often visualized as encompassing the human body, interacting directly with the energy system, including the chakras.

Interestingly, both the Merkaba and the chakra system emphasize the importance of balance. In chakra philosophy, the aim is to keep the energy centers aligned and in harmony. Similarly, the

Merkaba represents a state of equilibrium where the tetrahedral shapes spin in opposite directions, symbolizing the harmonious intersection of divine and earthly energies.

Kundalini: The Serpentine Force

Kundalini is another concept from Hindu philosophy that bears resemblance to the Merkaba. It refers to a form of primal energy located at the base of the spine. When awakened through specific practices, it ascends, activating the chakras and culminating in spiritual enlightenment. The ascent of kundalini energy mirrors the idea of the Merkaba being an ascension vehicle, a chariot of light that enables one to access higher spiritual dimensions.

Moreover, both kundalini and Merkaba practices involve intricate visualization and breathwork techniques. The 17-breath technique in Merkaba and the pranayama exercises in kundalini are strikingly parallel, aiming to awaken latent energy and induce states of expanded consciousness.

Mandalas: Geometries of the Spirit

In Buddhism and Hinduism, mandalas serve as spiritual symbols and tools for meditation. These intricate geometric designs symbolize the universe and are used to aid in concentration and spiritual growth. The Merkaba, too, is fundamentally a geometric shape, one that signifies the divine order and balance of the cosmos. The tetrahedral structure of the Merkaba can be likened to the complex geometric arrangements found in mandalas, both aiming to depict the structure and flow of cosmic energy.

Cultural Context Matters

While these similarities are fascinating, it's crucial to recognize that these concepts were formulated within different cultural and historical contexts. Chakras, kundalini, and mandalas have specific meanings and applications within their originating philosophies that may not be fully interchangeable with the concept of the Merkaba. For example, the Merkaba is often seen as a chariot for the soul, a concept that doesn't have a direct equivalent in Eastern philosophies.

Syncretism or Parallel Evolution?

One might wonder if these similarities are a result of cultural exchange or perhaps evidence of a universal spiritual understanding. Some scholars argue for syncretism, indicating a sharing of ideas among different spiritual traditions. Others suggest that these resemblances could be cases of parallel evolution, where different cultures independently develop similar spiritual concepts. However, no conclusive evidence supports either theory fully, making this a rich area for further study and contemplation.

In summary, the Merkaba's geometric and energetic qualities find echoes in Eastern spiritual traditions like the chakra system, kundalini energy, and the use of mandalas. While similarities abound, it's essential to appreciate these concepts in their unique cultural and philosophical settings. Whether these resemblances are due to a shared human spiritual experience or are mere coincidences remains a subject of scholarly debate. Nevertheless, the links between Merkaba and Eastern philosophies enrich our understanding of this mystical concept, offering additional avenues for exploration and practice.

CHAPTER 6: SACRED GEOMETRY AND SPIRITUALITY

Sacred geometry is sometimes referred to as the "architecture of the universe," and it is thought to be just as basic as mathematics in terms of its role in decoding the meaning of existence. It examines how shapes and patterns guide the structure of our world, both visible and invisible. In this chapter, we will explore how the Merkaba fits into this wider framework of sacred geometry, drawing connections with spirituality and deeper cosmic understanding.

The Role of Sacred Geometry in Spirituality

In spiritual traditions across the globe, sacred geometry is thought to symbolize the subtle energy patterns that make up the universe. In Hinduism and Buddhism, for example, the 'mandala' is a geometric design that represents the universe, and it's used as an aid in meditation to connect with the divine. Similarly, in Islamic art, intricate geometric designs reflect the infinite nature of God. In Christianity, the 'vesica piscis,' a shape made by intersecting two circles, has symbolic meanings, including the union of heaven and earth. These geometric patterns are not only aesthetically pleasing but are believed to be imbued with higher meanings and vibrations.

The Merkaba, a star tetrahedron, is a perfect example of sacred geometry in practice. The interlocking triangles that form the Merkaba are thought to represent the union between two opposite forces—masculine and feminine, heaven and earth, spirit and matter. Just like other elements of sacred geometry, the Merkaba is considered to be a two-way conduit: a symbol to understand the divine and a tool for the divine to act upon the world.

Correspondence with the Platonic Solids

In the realm of geometry, the five Platonic solids hold special significance. These are the tetrahedron, hexahedron (cube), octahedron, dodecahedron, and icosahedron. Each of these shapes is considered 'perfect' because every face, edge, and angle within each shape is identical. Ancient philosophers like Plato believed that these solids were the building blocks of the natural world. The tetrahedron, which forms the basis of the Merkaba, is one of these Platonic solids. Its presence in the Merkaba design adds a layer of metaphysical and geometric sanctity, often interpreted as a sign that this form is deeply embedded in the structure of the universe.

Resonance and Vibrations

Sacred geometry is not merely a visual or theoretical discipline; it's also about resonance and vibrations. According to spiritual practitioners, these shapes and patterns emit specific frequencies that can interact with the surrounding world and even with the human body's energy fields. Many advocates claim that by meditating on these shapes or by aligning oneself with their frequencies, it's possible to tap into higher realms of consciousness.

In the case of the Merkaba, the star tetrahedron is considered an extremely stable and harmonious form. When activated through meditation and visualization, it is believed to create a resonant field around the practitioner. While scientific evidence is still nascent in proving these claims, the enduring belief in the power of the Merkaba's shape offers compelling testimony for many.

The Flower of Life and Merkaba

One of the most iconic symbols related to sacred geometry is the Flower of Life, a pattern of multiple overlapping circles. This design can be seen in various ancient structures worldwide and is often linked to the formation of life itself. Within this complex pattern, the Merkaba shape can be extracted, giving it a unique position in the tapestry of existence as envisaged by sacred geometry. The incorporation of the Merkaba within the Flower of Life has led many to posit that understanding the Merkaba might be a key to unlocking deeper cosmic truths.

Philosophical Implications

At its core, the intersection of sacred geometry and spirituality suggests that the universe is not a random, chaotic expanse, but a carefully designed and intricately patterned entity. By studying these geometric forms, including the Merkaba, humanity has the opportunity to connect with deeper, universal laws. Whether considered from a religious perspective or a more spiritual standpoint, sacred geometry, and by extension the Merkaba, offers a bridge between the material world and the intangible realms of spirit and consciousness.

In summary, sacred geometry is a domain where mathematics, spirituality, and cosmology converge, offering symbols and patterns that have been revered across various cultural and spiritual traditions. The Merkaba, with its complex geometry and profound symbolism, aligns seamlessly with this ancient wisdom, offering a fascinating avenue for exploration and understanding. It serves as both a spiritual symbol and a cosmic tool, providing a geometric framework for understanding the universe's structure while resonating at frequencies believed to facilitate spiritual ascent.

CHAPTER 7: THE METAPHYSICAL ASPECT

The metaphysical realm often lies at the intersection of tangible reality and the more nebulous dimensions of consciousness, spirituality, and subjective experiences. Merkaba, with its geometric representation and spiritual significance, acts as a conduit between our physical world and the metaphysical. In this chapter, we shall explore how this ancient and intricate symbol connects us to realms beyond the material, particularly in terms of astral travel and the quest for enlightenment.

Astral Travel and Merkaba

Astral travel, also known as astral projection, refers to the experience of the "astral body" separating from the physical body to explore different planes of existence. Within many spiritual traditions, this is considered one of the ultimate experiences, a testament to the fluidity and multidimensionality of human consciousness.

When considering the Merkaba in the context of astral travel, the geometric form acts as a spiritual vehicle. The dual tetrahedrons, spinning in opposite directions, create an energy field. This energy field, many believe, is capable of carrying the astral body into other realms. Here, the Merkaba is not just a representation or a tool for meditation but becomes a functional component of metaphysical journeys. Its spinning action, like wheels of light, provides the momentum to traverse different layers of reality.

While scientific evidence supporting astral travel remains scant, countless anecdotes and traditional texts from diverse cultures corroborate the potential for such experiences. Whether the Merkaba acts as a metaphorical vessel or a literal one in these journeys is a matter of personal belief, but its recurrent association with astral experiences across cultures is certainly intriguing.

Enlightenment and the Merkaba

The quest for enlightenment, or a state of elevated awareness and communion with the divine, is another intriguing metaphysical aspect of the Merkaba. In Kabbalistic tradition, for instance, the Merkaba is often described as God's divine chariot, alluding to the mechanism by which human souls can ascend to higher states of consciousness.

When meditating with the Merkaba, practitioners often report experiences of profound insights, feelings of universal love, and a heightened sense of interconnectedness with all life forms. The Merkaba, in these contexts, serves as a cosmic elevator, allowing one to ascend through different layers of spiritual and emotional understanding until they reach a state of complete awareness or enlightenment.

Enlightenment, much like the Merkaba itself, is a concept that intersects multiple religious and spiritual traditions, each offering its own interpretation and methodology for achieving this exalted state. The common thread among these perspectives is the transformation of the individual from a state of ignorance or bounded consciousness to one of limitless understanding and compassion. In this transformative process, the Merkaba serves as both a guide and a facilitator, offering a geometric roadmap to these higher states of being.

Symbiosis of the Material and Metaphysical

A unique aspect of the Merkaba is how seamlessly it bridges the physical and the metaphysical. On one hand, its geometry can be measured, drawn, and modeled. On the other, its esoteric nature lends itself to explorations that defy conventional logic and empirical scrutiny. This dual nature makes the Merkaba a compelling focus for those interested in the marriage between the scientific and the spiritual.

Challenges and Skepticism

Of course, one cannot delve into the metaphysical without addressing the challenges and skepticism that come with it. Scientifically, neither astral travel nor enlightenment can be quantified or empirically verified, which places them in the realm of subjective experiences. Skeptics argue that experiences related to the Merkaba might be self-generated psychological phenomena rather than evidence of metaphysical realities.

However, the absence of empirical evidence does not necessarily negate the value or potential truth of these experiences. Metaphysical aspects like astral travel and enlightenment often occupy spaces that science has yet to map. Their exploration through the lens of Merkaba brings us face to face with the boundaries of human knowledge and understanding, encouraging us to question, seek, and perhaps, transcend.

To summarize, the metaphysical implications of the Merkaba are as fascinating as they are controversial. From its role in astral travel to its significance in the search for enlightenment, the Merkaba serves as a multi-dimensional tool that engages both our corporeal and spiritual existences. While science may yet have much to uncover about these realms, the cultural and personal testimonials about Merkaba's metaphysical aspects provide compelling avenues for exploration and, perhaps, a glimpse into the very nature of reality itself.

CHAPTER 8: PHYSICAL MANIFESTATION OF MERKABA ENERGY

Manifestation in Material Realms

While much of the previous discussion around Merkaba has focused on its metaphysical, spiritual, and mathematical aspects, there's a rich tapestry of stories, accounts, and reports claiming that Merkaba energy has had tangible, physical effects. Many practitioners of Merkaba meditation report experiencing sensory phenomena, including tingling sensations, changes in temperature, or even audible sounds during their practices. The question arises: Can this enigmatic concept, often reserved for spiritual or mystical exploration, actually manifest in the physical realm?

Sensory Phenomena

Anecdotal reports from practitioners claim various sensory experiences during their Merkaba meditations. These can range from tingling sensations in the fingers and toes to a feeling of light-headedness or warmth. Some even claim to hear subtle sounds or see auras around their bodies or within their closed-eye visual field. The credibility of such reports can vary widely, and it's challenging to subject these subjective experiences to rigorous scientific scrutiny. However, the consistency in descriptions across diverse cultures and practices can't be entirely discounted.

Energy Fields and Kirlian Photography

Kirlian photography, a technique that supposedly captures the "aura" or energy field around an object, has been used by some to offer evidence of Merkaba energy. Critics argue that the images are the result of simple electrical discharges, but proponents believe that these photographs reveal more. It is thought that the shape and color of these auras can reflect one's emotional or spiritual state, and some practitioners claim to see the Merkaba shape in these auras during specific meditations. While far from being definitive proof, the intersection of Merkaba symbolism and Kirlian photography remains an area of interest for many.

Reports of Healing

Perhaps the most impactful claims regarding the physical manifestation of Merkaba energy pertain to healing. While the scientific community remains skeptical due to the lack of controlled, peer-reviewed studies, numerous anecdotal accounts describe instances of accelerated healing, relief from chronic pain, or even the disappearance of tumors after engaging in Merkaba practices. These reports often emerge from holistic health circles and alternative medicine communities and should be approached cautiously until more robust evidence is available.

Investigating the Claims: A Scientific Lens

There have been preliminary studies conducted on the general effects of meditation and mindfulness on physical health, such as stress reduction, improved focus, and better emotional well-being. Still, specific research focusing on Merkaba is sparse.

Researchers face several challenges in this regard, from the complexity of designing experiments to measure "spiritual energy," to ethical concerns related to placebo effects. However, the existing literature on similar meditative practices can provide a starting point for future studies that aim to unpack the physical manifestation of Merkaba energy in a scientific manner.

Balancing Skepticism and Openness

Given the paucity of scientific evidence supporting the physical manifestations of Merkaba energy, a balanced approach is advisable. While it's essential to maintain a healthy level of skepticism, completely dismissing the testimonials and experiences of practitioners could mean turning a blind eye to phenomena not yet understood by science. After all, many scientific discoveries started as observations that were initially dismissed as anomalies. As interest in Merkaba and related spiritual practices grows, it's likely that the body of research will expand, offering new insights into these intriguing claims.

In summary, while accounts and reports suggest that Merkaba energy can manifest in various physical forms, from sensory experiences to possible healing effects, concrete scientific evidence remains elusive. The subjectivity inherent in these experiences makes them challenging to study in a standardized way. Nevertheless, the persistence of such reports across different cultures and spiritual practices suggests an underlying phenomenon worthy of further investigation. As science continues to evolve, one can only speculate whether the day will come when the physical manifestations of Merkaba energy can be measured, analyzed, and understood within the framework of empirical evidence.

CHAPTER 9: VISUALIZATION TECHNIQUES

Introduction

Visualization plays an integral role in accessing the potential of the Merkaba. After discussing its history, geometry, and physical manifestations, it is essential to touch upon how one can begin to engage with the Merkaba through visualization techniques. This chapter serves as a foundational guide to basic visualization practices aimed at helping beginners form a mental image of the Merkaba and activate its energies within themselves.

The Importance of Visualization in Merkaba Practices

Visualization is not a new concept in spiritual practices; it has been employed for centuries in various traditions. In the context of the Merkaba, visualization acts as a catalyst that helps manifest the geometric shape around the practitioner. This imaginary construct serves as a vessel for spiritual growth, healing, and even astral travel, as previously discussed in earlier chapters. While the techniques can range from basic to highly intricate, mastering the fundamentals is crucial for anyone aspiring to delve deeper into Merkaba practices.

Preparing for Visualization

Before you commence any visualization, setting the right environment can enhance the quality of your experience. Here are some general guidelines:

Physical Comfort: Choose a quiet space where you can sit or lie down comfortably. Physical ease can facilitate mental clarity.

Focused Mind: Spend a few minutes concentrating on your breath, driving away distractions. A calm mind is more receptive to visualization.

Intention Setting: Clearly define what you hope to achieve from this session. Whether it's emotional healing or spiritual enlightenment, having a purpose can guide your visualization process.

Basic Merkaba Visualization Technique

Begin with a Relaxed State: Close your eyes and take deep, calming breaths. Feel every part of your body relaxing, from your toes up to your head.

Rooting: Imagine roots extending from the base of your spine or feet, going deep into the Earth. Feel the grounding energy as you visualize these roots anchoring you securely.

Calling Energy: Imagine that a beam of pure white light descended from the heavens, passed through the top of your head, and flooded every part of your body with its illuminating radiance.

Forming the Tetrahedrons: Now, visualize two three-dimensional, four-sided pyramids (tetrahedrons) surrounding your body. One should be pointing upward and spinning clockwise, representing masculine energy. The other should be pointing downward and spinning counterclockwise, symbolizing feminine energy.

Merkaba Activation: Imagine these two tetrahedrons merging and forming a star tetrahedron around you. This star-like shape is your Merkaba.

Energizing the Merkaba: Envision your Merkaba glowing brighter with each breath you take, its spinning motion becoming more stable and harmonious.

Completion: When you feel your Merkaba is fully activated, slowly open your eyes and take a few moments to absorb the experience.

Tips for Enhancing Your Visualization

Color Associations: As you become more comfortable, you can begin to incorporate colors into your visualization. For instance, some practitioners associate the color green with healing energy and visualize a green glow around their Merkaba.

Sound Frequencies: Soft music or specific sound frequencies can also aid the visualization process by aligning your energetic vibration to the practice.

Summary

Visualization techniques are a foundational aspect of engaging with the Merkaba. The process begins with setting the right environment and state of mind, followed by a structured method to form and activate your Merkaba. As with any practice, consistency and sincerity in your efforts will yield a deeper connection with this ancient geometric chariot of light. With time and dedication, these foundational techniques can lead you to more advanced practices and profound spiritual experiences.

CHAPTER 10: ADVANCED VISUALIZATION

As you venture further into the world of Merkaba, the importance of visualization cannot be overstated. You've dipped your toes into the introductory methods; now it's time to wade deeper. Advanced visualization techniques offer a more immersive experience, allowing you to delve further into the intricacies of this mystic geometric form. In this chapter, we will explore how to enrich your Merkaba visualization with elements like colors, movements, and multi-sensory experiences.

Adding Colors to Your Merkaba Visualization

Colors are not just a feast for the eyes; they hold unique vibrations that correspond to different energies and states of being. For instance, while white light is often associated with purity, green might be linked to healing, and indigo to intuition. To incorporate color into your Merkaba visualization, begin by imagining your tetrahedrons in luminous shades. You could envision the male tetrahedron as a radiant blue and the female as a resplendent pink or any other colors that resonate with you. These vivid hues will not only make your practice more visually stimulating but can also help you tap into specific energies or intentions.

Dynamic Movements

Static visualizations have their merits, but introducing movement into your practice adds a layer of complexity and vigor. Picture your Merkaba's two tetrahedrons rotating in opposite directions—clockwise for the male, counter-clockwise for the female. This imagined rotation creates a dynamism that many believe facilitates the circulation of energies. In addition, such motion is thought to open up your Merkaba to higher frequencies, aiding in spiritual ascension and even multi-dimensional travel.

Multi-Sensory Integration

Advanced visualization also entails utilizing more than just your visual sense. Imagine the texture of the Merkaba's edges—are they smooth or etched with patterns? Can you feel its geometric perfection? Can you hear the subtle hum of energy emanating from its rotation, like a sacred hymn? Incorporating auditory or tactile sensations enhances the overall depth of your visualization. Some practitioners even suggest adding a fragrant dimension, such as picturing your Merkaba enveloped in the scent of lavender for relaxation or sandalwood for grounding.

Nested Merkabas

For those looking to take their practice even further, consider visualizing multiple Merkabas, or nested Merkabas. This concept, rooted in higher geometry, allows you to imagine Merkabas within Merkabas, each one smaller and rotating faster than the last. The idea is to generate a fractal energy pattern, thereby increasing the power and potential of your visualization.

Balancing Energies

As you get comfortable with advanced visualization, maintaining a balance between the different elements becomes crucial. This means ensuring that your focus on colors, movements, and sensory attributes doesn't overpower the foundational geometry of the Merkaba itself. A balanced approach helps you remain grounded while you explore the various facets of this intriguing shape.

Taking Your Time

Advanced visualization is not a sprint but a marathon, requiring patience and continual practice. Initially, you may find it challenging to maintain a clear mental image or to synchronize the movements and colors. It's alright. Progress in spiritual practice is often subtle and incremental. Don't rush the process; instead, cherish each moment of clarity or insight as a step closer to mastering this ancient art.

In summary, advanced visualization techniques offer a nuanced and multidimensional approach to understanding and experiencing the Merkaba. By infusing your practice with color, movement, and multi-sensory experiences, you not only enrich your engagement but potentially tap into deeper levels of consciousness and energy. Whether you're a seasoned practitioner or a curious novice ready to go the extra mile, these methods offer exciting possibilities for enhancing your Merkaba journey.

CHAPTER 11: BREATHING AND MEDITATION

Meditation and breath control are foundational practices in many spiritual traditions. When it comes to Merkaba, these elements can profoundly enhance your connection with this ancient symbol of sacred geometry. This chapter delves into how the discipline of controlled breathing and meditation complements your journey with the Merkaba. Here, we'll cover the role of breath in Merkaba meditation, its physiological and spiritual significance, and offer some breathing techniques to guide you.

The Breath and its Physiological Significance

The act of breathing is vital to human survival, serving as a bridge between the external and internal environments. Beyond physiological needs, breath has a deeper, spiritual significance. In yoga, the breath is often termed as "Prana," which means life force. In traditional Chinese practices, it is called "Qi" or "Chi," signifying the vital energy that flows through all things. Breath is more than a biological function; it can be a spiritual practice that governs the flow of energy within the body and mind.

Spiritual Significance of Breath in Merkaba Practice

In Merkaba practices, breath control is not just a physical function but a mechanism to achieve balance and harmony. Controlled breathing helps in aligning the spiritual, mental, and emotional states, which are essential for activating the Merkaba field around you. The quality of your breath can impact the vibrational frequency of your Merkaba, thereby influencing your ability to connect with higher dimensions. Just like the geometric shapes in the Merkaba are harmoniously balanced, your breath aims to create an internal balance, preparing you for a deeper spiritual experience.

The Pranayama Connection

Pranayama, an ancient yogic practice, focuses on breath control to enhance spiritual awakening and well-being. Many find similarities between Pranayama techniques and Merkaba breathwork, as both aim to balance and harness life force energy. In Merkaba, you engage in specialized breathing patterns, which may involve holding the breath, inhaling and exhaling through different nostrils, or utilizing diaphragmatic breathing. The intention is the same: to refine and direct your energy for spiritual elevation.

Breathing Techniques for Merkaba Activation

Activating your Merkaba field often involves a series of breaths coordinated with visualizations. Some common Merkaba breathing techniques are:

Inhalation and Counting: Deeply inhale, visualizing energy entering your body, and count to five or seven. Imagine this energy going down to the base of your spine and spreading throughout your body.

Breath Holding and Visualization: Hold your breath and visualize a sphere of light forming around you. Focus on connecting this light to the geometric shapes of your Merkaba.

Exhalation and Release: As you exhale, imagine all the negative energy leaving your body, making room for positive life force energy.

Incorporating Meditation

Breathing is often the starting point for deeper meditation practices. Once you've attained a balanced state through breathing, you can venture into more advanced Merkaba visualizations. Meditation can help you become more receptive to the energies around you, making it easier to align with your Merkaba. Whether you opt for mindfulness meditation, transcendental meditation, or a Merkaba-specific guided meditation, the key is to maintain your focus and openness.

Integrating Breathing and Meditation with Advanced Visualization

If you've already mastered the basics of Merkaba visualization as discussed in previous chapters, you can integrate breathing and meditation for a more advanced experience. For instance, as you breathe in, you might visualize energy spiraling around the Merkaba's tetrahedrons. As you hold your breath, you can envision this energy forming a cohesive shield around you. And as you exhale, visualize connecting with higher frequencies or dimensions.

In summary, the discipline of controlled breathing and meditation is crucial for enhancing your Merkaba practice.

Through specific techniques and conscious efforts, you can direct and balance the energy within you, providing a fertile ground for deeper spiritual exploration. Whether you are a novice or have considerable experience with the Merkaba, integrating these elements can make your journey much more enriching and enlightening.

CHAPTER 12: RIDING THE LIGHT CHARIOT: PERSONAL EXPERIENCES

The transformative potential of Merkaba often takes shape through individual experiences. While theory and techniques offer the framework, stories of personal journeys paint a vivid landscape that illuminates the profound effects of Merkaba meditation. In this chapter, we delve into an anthology of testimonies and narratives from individuals who have had unique encounters with the Merkaba. Their stories offer insightful perspectives, from spiritual revelations to tangible shifts in well-being.

Encounters with Inner Peace

Emma, a yoga instructor from California, recalled her first encounter with Merkaba as a "healing experience." Struggling with anxiety for many years, she decided to integrate Merkaba meditation into her daily routine. Within weeks, Emma noticed a marked decrease in her anxiety levels. "It was like I'd accessed a sanctuary within myself that I didn't know existed," she said. For Emma, the Merkaba became more than a geometric construct; it became a space of mental peace and solace.

Expanding Conscious Awareness

Martin, a philosophy professor, was intrigued by the concept of the Merkaba's role in expanding consciousness. Over the course of several months of dedicated Merkaba meditation, he found a heightened sense of awareness not just spiritually but also in his day-to-day activities. "Things I'd once overlooked appeared luminous and significant. It felt as if a veil had been lifted," Martin explained. He drew connections between his enhanced mindfulness and ancient philosophical ideas, realizing that his experience with Merkaba had grounded these abstract notions in a tangible reality.

Physical Well-being and Healing Energy

Selena, a holistic health practitioner, decided to explore the Merkaba after encountering it in various healing modalities. Suffering from chronic pain, she started to incorporate Merkaba visualization techniques into her existing regimen of treatments. To her surprise, her pain levels significantly decreased over a period of three months. "I wouldn't say it's a magical cure, but I could literally feel the energy circulating and rejuvenating my physical body," she said. Selena continues to use Merkaba meditation as an adjunct to her health regimen.

Astral Projection and Multi-dimensional Travel

Richard, a software engineer with a penchant for esoteric sciences, approached the Merkaba with an eye towards its promises of astral projection and multi-dimensional travel. A skeptic by nature, Richard meticulously documented his Merkaba meditation experiences. After several attempts, he reported instances of out-of-body experiences that he found both disorienting and enlightening. "It was a strange blend of feeling both detached and profoundly connected with the universe," he stated. Richard is one of many who claim to have experienced the Merkaba as a vehicle for exploring the more mysterious realms of existence.

The Collective Experience

Jenny and her meditation group in Vermont engaged in collective Merkaba practices. The collective experience, according to Jenny, was uniquely uplifting. "It felt as though our individual Merkabas were intertwining, creating a radiant and powerful energy field that was greater than the sum of its parts," she explained. Jenny's group claimed to feel a profound sense of unity and interconnectedness, a testament to the Merkaba's potential in fostering collective consciousness.

Summary

From the alleviation of psychological burdens to the exploration of uncharted realms of consciousness, personal encounters with the Merkaba span a vast spectrum. These stories are vital testimonials that enrich our understanding of what the Merkaba can offer. While the experiences are deeply personal, they collectively serve as a mosaic that adds color, depth, and nuance to the intricate tapestry of Merkaba mysticism. As you read these stories, consider how your own journey with the Merkaba might unfold, and what unique narrative you could contribute to this ever-evolving field.

CHAPTER 13: DANGERS AND MISUNDERSTANDINGS

While the journey through Merkaba mysticism is one imbued with potential for enlightenment, spiritual growth, and even purported multi-dimensional travel, it is also fraught with certain pitfalls and misunderstandings. These risks not only stem from inaccuracies and lack of knowledge but also from improper practice and a lack of ethical consideration. This chapter aims to address these issues in order to prepare you for a safer and more rewarding Merkaba experience.

Incorrect Visualization Techniques

When engaging in Merkaba meditation, one of the most crucial elements is the accurate visualization of its complex geometry. Incorrect visualization can lead to a distorted experience, nullifying the spiritual benefits one seeks to gain. Moreover, erroneous visualization can induce mental strain and confusion. Some practitioners report increased levels of anxiety and feelings of disorientation when they misalign their visualizations, particularly during the advanced stages of Merkaba practice.

Ignoring the Breath

Breathing, in the context of Merkaba meditation, is not just a physiological necessity but a gateway to controlling and channeling the energy flow within one's own Merkaba. Ignoring the prescribed breathing techniques or failing to synchronize the breath with one's visualizations can lead to an ineffective practice. While Merkaba is a largely benign spiritual exercise, inconsistent breathing can lead to discomfort, such as dizziness or shortness of breath, and hamper the meditative state you aim to achieve.

Ethical Lapses

As with any spiritual endeavor, the practice of Merkaba carries its own set of ethical considerations. Incorrect practices that include, but are not limited to, manipulating others through Merkaba energy or using it for malevolent purposes can not only negate any spiritual progress but could also introduce negative energy into one's life. The principle of "what you send out, you attract back" is an often-cited axiom in various spiritual traditions and holds true here as well.

Overestimating Scientific Validation

While it's tantalizing to consider the scientific explanations for Merkaba and its associated phenomena, it's crucial to remember that research is still in its nascent stage. There's a danger of over-relying on partial or incomplete scientific theories to validate one's own spiritual experiences. Such attitudes can lead to misinterpretation of both scientific data and personal spiritual experiences, leaving one with a skewed understanding of the Merkaba.

Inauthentic Sources and False Gurus

The rise of the digital age has been a double-edged sword for the Merkaba community. While it has facilitated the spread of knowledge, it has also given rise to numerous inauthentic sources and self-proclaimed gurus. Engaging with these deceptive individuals or relying on their incorrect teachings can have a variety of negative consequences, from wasted time and resources to the potential risk of spiritual or emotional harm. It is thus crucial to approach this practice with discernment and to source your information from credible, well-respected avenues.

Summary

Navigating the realm of Merkaba involves more than just knowing the right techniques; it's equally crucial to be aware of the dangers and misunderstandings that one may encounter. Whether it's faulty visualization techniques, ignoring breathing patterns, ethical missteps, or misplaced faith in incomplete scientific theories, these pitfalls can derail your spiritual journey. Being well-informed is the first step towards a fulfilling Merkaba experience. Always approach your practice with humility, ethical integrity, and a sense of lifelong learning to get the most out of what Merkaba mysticism has to offer.

CHAPTER 14: THE 17-BREATH TECHNIQUE

The 17-Breath Technique is an indispensable practice in the world of Merkaba meditation. As we have seen in previous chapters, Merkaba is more than just a geometric figure; it's a complex system of beliefs and practices that delve into the metaphysical realms, the geometry of the soul, and the potential for interdimensional travel. Understanding and applying the 17-Breath Technique is like receiving the keys to a powerful vehicle—one that is said to transport you not just through space, but also through dimensions of consciousness. This chapter offers an in-depth look into this pivotal technique, its origins, its steps, and the profound implications it has for your Merkaba practice.

Origins of the 17-Breath Technique

The 17-Breath Technique finds its roots in various ancient traditions, including Kabbalistic teachings and early Eastern philosophies. It's believed that the essence of this practice was known to ancient mystics and spiritual leaders but kept as an esoteric secret. Over time, these techniques were adapted and modernized to make them more accessible for contemporary practitioners. The 17-breath cycle aims to activate the Merkaba field around an individual, harnessing what many believe to be innate human potential for spiritual ascension and enlightenment.

The Basic Mechanics

At its core, the 17-Breath Technique is a sequence of breaths combined with specific mental visualizations and physical postures. While the basic mechanics involve inhaling and exhaling, it's far from ordinary respiration. Each of the 17 breaths corresponds to a particular focus and intention, often linked with the body's chakra system, sacred geometry, or other metaphysical concepts. For example, one breath might focus on grounding the practitioner to the Earth, while another might concentrate on opening the heart chakra. Each breath serves as a stepping-stone toward achieving a heightened state of consciousness.

Steps Involved

While the 17-Breath Technique is intricate, a few general steps are involved in this practice:

Preliminary Grounding: Prior to initiating the 17 breaths, take a few moments to ground yourself, often by focusing on your connection to the Earth or by centering your awareness in the present moment.

Activating Breath: This is usually the first in the series of 17 breaths, and it is intended to awaken the prana or life force within you.

Chakra Alignment Breath: Focusing on aligning the chakras usually follows, preparing the energy centers of the body for the activations to come.

Sequential Ascension: Subsequent breaths focus on various aspects like activating the tetrahedral energy fields, enhancing spiritual vision, and solidifying your connection to higher realms.

Completion and Integration: The final breaths are aimed at completing the activation of the Merkaba field and integrating the newly aligned energies into your physical and metaphysical being.

It's essential to note that the above are generalized steps and variations may exist, depending on the specific tradition or teacher you are following.

Benefits and Precautions

Practitioners who have faithfully applied the 17-Breath Technique often report heightened states of awareness, increased intuitive abilities, and even experiences that could be categorized as mystical or transcendental. However, it's crucial to approach this practice with due diligence and care. Incorrect application could potentially result in energy imbalances or psychological distress. As discussed in Chapter 13 about the dangers and misunderstandings, it's advisable to learn this technique under the guidance of a qualified instructor, especially if you are a beginner in the realm of Merkaba meditation.

The Profound Implications

The 17-Breath Technique is more than just a meditation practice; for many, it's a transformative life practice. Engaging with these breaths often implies a commitment to a lifelong journey of spiritual discovery and personal development. Beyond the immediate effects that practitioners may experience, this technique symbolizes the union of ancient wisdom and modern interpretation, a blend of the mystical and the practical, a marriage of the earthly and the divine.

In summary, the 17-Breath Technique is often considered the nucleus of Merkaba meditation. It is a well-coordinated sequence of breaths, visualizations, and intentions that serve as the activation mechanism for your Merkaba—the light chariot that offers the promise of elevating your spiritual experience. Whether you are new to Merkaba or a seasoned practitioner, integrating this technique into your practice could provide not just a deeper understanding of this ancient system, but a pathway to realms of consciousness that have fascinated humans for millennia.

CHAPTER 15: MERKABA AND HEALING

In this chapter, we delve into the intriguing subject of how the Merkaba, often described as a light chariot or a geometric representation of the human soul, intersects with the concept of healing. Specifically, we explore how this ancient symbol has been integrated into various holistic health practices to potentially offer physical, emotional, and spiritual wellness.

The Healing Potential of Merkaba

The notion of the Merkaba's role in healing is primarily rooted in metaphysical and spiritual traditions, where it is viewed as a mechanism that can channel and focus energy. According to practitioners, the Merkaba is believed to resonate with the natural frequency of the universe, allowing for the transfer of universal life force or "chi" into the individual or object it surrounds. This life force is said to possess healing properties that can address ailments both of the body and the mind.

However, it's crucial to note that while there are numerous anecdotal claims and personal testimonies regarding Merkaba-assisted healing, these are not yet supported by empirical scientific evidence. Hence, Merkaba's role in healing is best considered complementary to traditional medical practices rather than a substitute.

Energy Flow and Chakras

The Merkaba has often been discussed in conjunction with the chakra system, particularly in Eastern spiritual philosophies. The chakras are considered energy centers within the body, and practitioners assert that a well-aligned and activated Merkaba can effectively channel energy to these centers. By doing so, it may help in balancing the chakras, thereby promoting better health and emotional well-being.

The process typically involves meditation and visualization exercises where one imagines the Merkaba enveloping their body. During these meditative states, the Merkaba is visualized as spinning, and this spinning action is thought to create a flow of energy that can interact with the chakras. It is hypothesized that this interaction can help clear energy blockages, align the chakras, and enhance the body's innate ability to heal itself.

Holistic Health Applications

The idea of Merkaba-assisted healing has found its way into various holistic health practices. For instance, in Reiki, a Japanese form of energy healing, practitioners sometimes incorporate Merkaba visualization to enhance the flow of energy. Additionally, in practices like acupuncture and crystal healing, the Merkaba is sometimes used as a symbol to focus intention and channel healing energy more efficiently.

These practices often focus on the concept of "wholeness," where healing is not just the absence of disease but also entails a balanced emotional and spiritual state. In this context, the

Merkaba is seen as a tool that aids in achieving this state of complete well-being.

Caveats and Ethical Concerns

As with any alternative or complementary healing modality, it is crucial to approach Merkaba-assisted healing with caution and an informed perspective. Misuse or misunderstanding of these techniques can lead to adverse effects. For example, focusing too much on Merkaba meditation without addressing medical conditions through conventional means can lead to deterioration in health. Ethically, practitioners should disclose that while the concept of Merkaba-assisted healing is steeped in tradition and personal experiences, it lacks broad scientific validation.

Summary

The concept of Merkaba in the realm of healing provides a fascinating blend of geometry, spirituality, and holistic health. While the scientific backing for Merkaba-assisted healing is still lacking, its incorporation into various spiritual and holistic practices indicates a sustained belief in its healing potential. It serves as a complementary tool that aims to promote overall well-being by purportedly channeling universal life force energy into the body. However, like all complementary therapies, it should be approached with caution and as an adjunct to, not a replacement for, traditional medical care.

CHAPTER 16: THE SCIENCE BEHIND THE MYSTICISM

In a book that traverses ancient wisdom, sacred geometry, and spiritual insights, it's tempting to pigeonhole the concept of Merkaba as purely mystical or metaphysical. However, a comprehensive understanding demands a multifaceted approach. In this chapter, we delve into scientific perspectives that may provide explanations—or at least correlations—for some aspects of Merkaba.

The Geometry of the Merkaba and Mathematical Reality

The tetrahedral structure of the Merkaba is not a random choice; it's grounded in mathematics and geometry, disciplines that science holds in high regard. In Platonic solids, a key element in geometry, the tetrahedron is the simplest form and represents the element of fire in ancient symbolic systems. The interconnectedness of geometry and natural phenomena is also a topic of scientific research. Studies in fractal geometry, for example, show how simple mathematical formulas can create complex structures much like those in nature, such as snowflakes or leaves. While not a direct explanation of the Merkaba, this does demonstrate how fundamental geometric shapes could potentially be integral to the very fabric of the universe.

Biofield Resonance and the Energy Fields

In the world of quantum physics, the idea of a biofield—energy fields that are thought to both emanate from living bodies and to encapsulate them—has been gaining traction. While mainstream science remains cautious in accepting this concept, numerous peer-reviewed articles have studied biofield therapies and their effectiveness. The conceptual similarity between the Merkaba's energy fields and scientific understanding of biofields is striking, though we should approach it as correlation rather than causation at this stage.

Merkaba and Quantum Entanglement

Quantum physics introduces the concept of entanglement, where particles are so deeply connected that the state of one instantly influences the state of another, regardless of distance. This phenomenon has been experimentally confirmed, and while it doesn't directly confirm the existence of Merkaba fields, it opens up intriguing possibilities. Could the instantaneous shifts in energy or consciousness reported in Merkaba practices be some form of macroscopic quantum entanglement? Again, this is speculative but poses a fascinating line of inquiry.

Studies in Human Consciousness

There is increasing interest within the scientific community in understanding the nature of consciousness. Research in neurology and psychology tries to decode how the brain produces awareness and how altered states of consciousness occur. Meditation, which is a key component of Merkaba practice, has been extensively studied for its effects on the brain and consciousness. Neuroimaging studies show that regular meditation practices can change neural pathways and even affect areas of the brain related to awareness. Could Merkaba meditation produce specific, measurable changes in brain function? The evidence suggests this is a fruitful area for future research.

Challenges in Scientific Exploration

It's essential to note that while these scientific paradigms may offer some avenues for understanding Merkaba, the exploration is fraught with challenges. Mystical and spiritual experiences are often subjective and do not easily lend themselves to empirical measurement. Furthermore, existing scientific methodologies might not be adequately equipped to explore phenomena that are rooted in different philosophical premises. Thus, while science can offer additional perspectives, it cannot be the sole yardstick by which Merkaba or any other spiritual practice is understood or validated.

Summary

While the concept of Merkaba has its roots in ancient spirituality and mysticism, various elements resonate intriguingly with modern scientific thought. From the geometric principles underpinning its structure to quantum theories that could potentially explain its energetic properties, there are multiple avenues for a science-based exploration of Merkaba. However, the complex, multi-dimensional nature of the subject means that scientific investigation can complement but not replace a holistic understanding. The essence of Merkaba, like many spiritual practices, lies in the convergence of diverse perspectives, including, but not limited to, scientific inquiry.

CHAPTER 17: THE MERKABA AND QUANTUM PHYSICS

In this chapter, we delve into the intriguing intersection between the spiritual concept of Merkaba and the scientific realm of quantum physics. The aim is to explore how modern scientific theories could potentially shed light on the ancient, mystical phenomena associated with Merkaba.

Quantum Mechanics: A Brief Overview

Quantum mechanics is a branch of physics that deals with phenomena on an extremely small scale, usually subatomic particles like electrons, photons, and quarks. The principles of quantum mechanics defy our intuitive understanding of the world, often seeming bizarre and counterintuitive. Concepts such as superposition, in which particles can exist in several states simultaneously, and entanglement, in which particles can be "linked" despite being separated by huge distances, have fundamental consequences for our understanding of reality.

Quantum Consciousness and Merkaba

Among the theories in quantum physics is the hypothesis of quantum consciousness, which suggests that consciousness arises from quantum processes within the brain. Although this idea is still the subject of ongoing research and debate, some scholars and spiritual practitioners have started to draw parallels between the concept of quantum consciousness and the Merkaba. The Merkaba, often described as a "light chariot" for the soul, could be seen as a quantum vehicle of sorts, facilitating states of higher consciousness, just as quantum particles exist in states of superposition.

The Double-Slit Experiment and Observer Effect

One of the most famous experiments in quantum physics is the double-slit experiment, which demonstrates that particles can act as both particles and waves, depending on whether they are observed. This has led to discussions around the role of consciousness in shaping reality, a point that resonates deeply with Merkaba practices that use focused intention and visualization. Could it be that the Merkaba is a form of "conscious geometry," shaped by our intentions and perceptions? While no conclusive evidence supports this claim, it is an intriguing area for future study.

Entanglement and Spiritual Connection

The concept of quantum entanglement could offer a scientific metaphor for the spiritual connectivity often attributed to Merkaba practices. Entangled particles remain connected, mirroring each other's states instantaneously, regardless of the distance that separates them. Similarly, the Merkaba is often said to facilitate a profound sense of interconnectedness, uniting the individual soul with the larger, collective soul or higher dimensions. This sense of "quantum spirituality" opens up new avenues for understanding the deep connections that Merkaba practitioners often report.

Limitations and Cautions

While the intersections between quantum physics and Merkaba spirituality are tantalizing, it's crucial to approach them with caution. Correlation does not imply causation, and speculative connections between the two should not be considered definitive proof of any spiritual or scientific principle. Moreover, quantum physics is an evolving field, and many of its theories are still under examination. Therefore, while the potential for a groundbreaking synthesis between Merkaba spirituality and quantum mechanics is enticing, it remains a subject of research and should be interpreted cautiously.

In summary, the realm of quantum physics offers a host of concepts that tantalizingly intersect with the spiritual practice and understanding of the Merkaba. From the mysteries of quantum consciousness to the bizarre implications of the double-slit experiment and quantum entanglement, there are numerous avenues where science and spirituality might meet and enrich each other. While definitive evidence linking the Merkaba and quantum physics is yet to be found, the potential for a meaningful dialogue between these two realms continues to ignite curiosity and inspire both scientific and spiritual explorations.

CHAPTER 18: BUILDING A MERKABA: PHYSICAL MODELS

Creating a physical model of the Merkaba can serve as an invaluable aid for meditation and visualization practices. As you have been following along, you already understand that the Merkaba is a complex geometric shape, essentially two interlocking tetrahedra. One faces upwards, channeling the energies of the heavens, while the other points downwards, drawing from the Earth. In this chapter, we'll guide you through the steps to construct your own Merkaba model, discuss the materials that can be used, and explore how having a tangible representation can enhance your Merkaba experience.

Choosing the Right Material

Your choice of material will depend on your personal preferences, as well as what you aim to achieve with your Merkaba practice. Here are some commonly used materials:

Wood: A natural and organic choice, wooden models can be carved or assembled.

Metal: Usually made of brass or copper, metal models are more durable but can be heavier.

Crystal: Often considered the most spiritually resonant, but can be fragile.

3D Printed: Made from a variety of materials, these models can be custom-designed but may lack the natural essence.

Creating a Wooden Merkaba

If you opt for a wooden Merkaba, you will need wooden dowels or rods, glue, and perhaps some tools for carving or sanding. The essential steps are as follows:

Cut six equal-length dowels for each tetrahedron.

Arrange three dowels into a triangle and glue the ends.

Repeat for the other triangle.

Interlock the two triangles and secure them with glue.

Once your wooden model is complete, you can paint it, varnish it, or leave it natural, depending on your aesthetic preferences.

Assembling a Metal Merkaba

Metal Merkabas often come in the form of kits that you can assemble yourself. However, if you're adept at metalwork, you can certainly craft one from scratch. The steps for assembly are similar to those for the wooden model, though you'll need to use soldering or welding techniques to join the pieces securely.

Crafting a Crystal Merkaba

Creating a crystal Merkaba requires a bit more care and precision, given the fragility of the material. Pre-cut crystal pieces can be purchased for assembly, but joining them requires a specialized adhesive designed for crystal or glass. Ensure your workspace is free of clutter and distractions, and wear protective gear if needed.

The 3D Printed Option

The technology available for 3D printing now makes it possible to create accurate and individualized Merkaba models. You have a selection of options available to you in terms of the material, color, and size of the item, and even the design. Websites and online communities often offer downloadable templates, which you can then modify to your liking.

The Benefits of a Physical Model

Having a physical Merkaba model can be a powerful tool for both beginners and those advanced in Merkaba meditations. It serves as a visual and tactile focal point during practices, helping to enhance concentration and understanding of this complex geometric form. Further, it can act as a constant reminder of the interconnectedness between the human soul and the universe, grounding your practice in the physical realm even as you explore the metaphysical.

To summarize, building a physical Merkaba model can be a rewarding endeavor that enriches your understanding and practice of Merkaba meditation. Whether you choose wood, metal, crystal, or a 3D printed version, the process of creation is itself a form of meditation and connection with this ancient, geometric symbol. May your new Merkaba model serve as a vibrant conduit for both earthly and celestial energies.

CHAPTER 19: MERKABA AND MUSIC

The interplay between sound and spirituality is as ancient as human history itself. Various cultures, religions, and spiritual practices have long considered music and sound as powerful catalysts in reaching states of higher consciousness, healing, or mystical experiences. In the same vein, the relationship between Merkaba meditation and music forms a fascinating nexus that invites further exploration. Sound isn't merely an auditory experience; it has the potential to be a transformative force in our meditative practices. This chapter delves into how music can enrich your Merkaba meditative experience, offering both theoretical perspectives and practical insights.

The Sound of Sacred Geometry

The Merkaba, as we have discussed in previous chapters, is intricately connected to sacred geometry. The mathematics and proportions found in its structure parallel those found in nature and even music theory. In classical terms, the concept of the "Music of the Spheres" posits that celestial bodies, like planets and stars, produce harmonic resonances. This idea extends into modern thinking, where fractal patterns and Fibonacci sequences appear not only in physical forms but also in musical scales and harmonies.

Vibrational Frequencies and Energy Fields

One of the key points of convergence between Merkaba and music lies in the realm of vibrational frequencies. Sound is essentially a form of energy vibration that travels through a medium, such as air or water. The Merkaba, too, is often described as an energy field or a sort of "light vehicle" comprised of interlocking tetrahedra, which also vibrates at certain frequencies. There is growing interest in how sound frequencies can interact with the human energy field, potentially aligning or enhancing it. Some practitioners advocate the use of particular frequencies—often termed "Solfeggio frequencies"—to activate or work with the Merkaba. While there isn't scientific consensus on this, the subjective experiences of many suggest a significant impact.

Therapeutic Potentials of Sound

The therapeutic impact of sound and music is another area of congruence with Merkaba practices. Various forms of sound therapy like binaural beats, Tibetan singing bowls, and gong baths have been cited for their potential healing benefits, from stress reduction to improved mental clarity. In Merkaba meditation, which also has a strong focus on healing and energy manipulation, incorporating sound can add another layer to the practice. Some people find that specific types of music or soundscapes aid them in reaching deeper states of concentration, facilitating a more profound meditative experience.

Practical Considerations: Music Selection and Integration

If you're interested in incorporating music into your Merkaba practices, here are some considerations:

Choose music or sounds that you find calming or uplifting. The intention is to facilitate a meditative state, not distract from it.

Pay attention to tempo. Slower rhythms are generally more conducive to relaxation and focus.

Experiment with different types of sound. Nature sounds, ambient music, or specific frequencies may all offer unique benefits.

Consider the volume. It should be loud enough to be immersive but not so loud as to be jarring or unsettling.

The Confluence of Sound and Silence

While music can offer a powerful accompaniment to Merkaba meditation, it's also essential to honor the role of silence. Silence provides the space for internal reflection, allowing you to fully engage with your inner experiences without external distraction. Many practitioners opt for a balanced approach, using music to enter a meditative state and then embracing periods of silence to deepen their focus on the Merkaba visualization.

In summary, the marriage of Merkaba meditation and music opens up a world of possibilities for enriching your spiritual practice. Whether through aligning vibrational frequencies, enhancing focus, or adding a healing dimension, sound can be an instrumental part of your journey with the Merkaba. Just like each note in a melody, the role of music in this context is part of a larger symphony of spiritual growth, self-discovery, and cosmic exploration.

CHAPTER 20: CRYSTALS AND THE MERKABA

Crystals have fascinated humanity for ages, not just for their beauty but also for their purported metaphysical properties. In the realm of Merkaba meditation and practices, crystals are often considered conduits that can amplify or balance energies. This chapter delves into the intriguing relationship between crystals and the Merkaba, examining how these natural formations can be integrated into Merkaba meditations and their potential effects on the practitioner.

The Metaphysical Properties of Crystals

Many ancient cultures, including those of Egypt, Greece, and India, have associated specific powers with various types of crystals. Whether it's rose quartz for love, amethyst for spiritual growth, or clear quartz for amplifying energy, each crystal is believed to have a unique vibrational frequency. These frequencies resonate with human energy fields and can thus be utilized to enhance specific aspects of the Merkaba experience. For example, using a crystal associated with grounding like hematite might help stabilize the base of your Merkaba, whereas a higher vibration crystal like selenite could be used to connect more readily with higher realms.

Synergy with Sacred Geometry

Crystals themselves are a remarkable demonstration of sacred geometry in nature. They form in geometric patterns at the molecular level, often mirroring the Platonic Solids, a set of five 3D shapes that are foundational to sacred geometry. In Merkaba practices, the Platonic Solids are of particular importance as they relate to the geometric structure of the Merkaba itself, which is a star tetrahedron. Integrating crystals into your Merkaba meditation can be seen as harmonizing one form of sacred geometry with another, setting the stage for an intensified energetic experience.

Crystal Grids and the Merkaba

Creating a crystal grid around your physical space while meditating with the Merkaba can establish a powerful energy field. Typically, a grid consists of multiple crystals laid out in a geometric pattern, often reflecting the same sacred geometry that underpins the Merkaba. The grid serves as a catalyst that enhances your focus and intent, whether it's for healing, spiritual growth, or other objectives. The central crystal in the grid can be programmed with your intention, serving as the focal point that draws in and amplifies the energy from the surrounding crystals and aligns it with your Merkaba.

Selecting and Preparing Crystals

Choosing the right crystals for your Merkaba meditation can be an intimate process. Trust your intuition and see which crystals resonate with you. Once chosen, it's crucial to cleanse them of any residual energies. Methods for cleansing include smudging with sage, placing them under the moonlight, or bathing them in saltwater. After cleansing, you can charge your crystals by setting an intention for them or meditating with them prior to their use in Merkaba practices.

Cautionary Notes

While the use of crystals can enhance your Merkaba experience, it's crucial to exercise discernment. Some crystals have strong energies that may not be suitable for everyone. Always make sure to read up on the properties of each crystal and possibly consult with experienced practitioners or guides. Additionally, crystals should not replace medical advice or treatment; they are a complementary spiritual tool.

Summary

The integration of crystals into Merkaba practices offers a fascinating avenue for enriching your spiritual journey. Their inherent geometric patterns and unique vibrational frequencies can synergize beautifully with the sacred geometry of the Merkaba. Through careful selection, cleansing, and programming, these natural gemstones can become potent allies, amplifying your intentions and enhancing your meditative experiences. However, as with any spiritual tool, it's important to approach the use of crystals with informed caution and respect for their potent energies.

CHAPTER 21: THE DIGITAL AGE OF MERKABA

As we navigate the complex tapestry of Merkaba's history, spirituality, and geometrical significance, it's impossible to ignore the impact of technology on our understanding and experience of this ancient concept. While it might seem paradoxical to bring the digital world into a conversation rooted deeply in ancient wisdom and spirituality, modern technology provides tools that can aid in grasping the nuances of the Merkaba and even facilitate a more vivid experiential understanding. In this chapter, we'll explore the digital frontiers that have opened up new avenues for engaging with the Merkaba, such as virtual reality, computer simulations, and online communities.

Virtual Reality and Immersive Experiences

Virtual Reality (VR) is one of the most promising technologies when it comes to creating an immersive experience of the Merkaba. Traditionally, the practice of visualizing the Merkaba involves meditation and sometimes even guided group practices to understand the geometric shapes and movements of the Merkaba field around you. However, VR can create an environment where you can see and almost feel the complex geometric shapes, their rotations, and the energy flows, thus adding a new dimension to the visualization techniques we discussed in earlier chapters.

Using VR headsets, one can enter a 3D simulation of the Merkaba, exploring its tetrahedral geometry from different angles and perspectives. Moreover, these virtual experiences can be programmed to represent the Merkaba's movement, allowing for a better understanding of the complex rotations that are often difficult to grasp in mental visualizations alone.

Computer Simulations and Modeling

Apart from virtual reality, computer simulations and software 1modelling tools also offer educational insights into the Merkaba's geometry. Advanced software can break down the Merkaba's structure into simpler components, explaining the mathematical principles behind each aspect. Such tools are invaluable for those who aim to understand the Merkaba not just as a spiritual or metaphysical entity but also as a geometrical marvel. Researchers and scientists exploring the scientific aspects of Merkaba, as touched upon in earlier chapters, can use these simulations for a variety of exploratory studies.

Online Communities and Shared Experiences

The Internet has democratized information like never before. As a result, numerous online forums, social media groups, and websites are dedicated to discussions around the Merkaba. From sharing personal experiences to disseminating new research and developments, these platforms provide a meeting ground for both novices and experts. While the experience of Merkaba is profoundly personal, the collective wisdom and shared insights found in these online communities can be invaluable in deepening your understanding and practice. The testimonies, shared visualization techniques, and even warnings about potential pitfalls make these platforms an essential part of the modern Merkaba landscape.

Apps and Digital Tools for Practice

Several mobile applications and digital tools have been designed to aid in the practice of Merkaba meditation and visualization. These apps often come with guided audio or visual aids, and some even incorporate biofeedback technology to gauge your level of relaxation or focus. The integration of these technologies aims to provide a more streamlined and effective approach to Merkaba practices. While they may never replace the depth achieved through traditional methods, they serve as accessible entry points or supplementary aids for practitioners.

Ethical Considerations in the Digital Age

While the digital era brings an array of tools and platforms to enhance our understanding and experience of Merkaba, it's essential to approach them with discernment. The commodification of spirituality is a genuine concern, and not all apps, VR experiences, or online forums are created with the authentic intent of fostering spiritual growth or understanding. It's crucial to research and perhaps consult credible sources or teachers before fully integrating these digital resources into your practice.

In summary, the digital age has both expanded and complicated our engagement with the Merkaba. Virtual reality and computer simulations offer unprecedented perspectives into its geometric complexity, online communities provide shared wisdom and experiences, and digital tools offer more accessible ways to engage in practice. However, as we integrate these new tools, let's also remain vigilant about the ethical considerations that come with the digitization of an ancient spiritual concept.

CHAPTER 22: THE COLLECTIVE MERKABA

The exploration of the Merkaba thus far has primarily focused on individual experiences and practices. However, a captivating dimension of this ancient and multifaceted concept is the idea of a "Collective Merkaba." In this chapter, we will delve into the notion that a group of individuals can, in theory, come together to form a collective Merkaba, amplifying its effects and potential applications.

The Notion of Collective Consciousness

The idea of collective consciousness, which is a word that refers to shared beliefs and moral attitudes that function as a unifying force across society, is profoundly ingrained in the Merkaba. In religious and spiritual traditions worldwide, from Vedic philosophies to indigenous practices, the power of communal prayer, meditation, or intention-setting is often emphasized. By aligning individual energies and intentions, a more potent force is believed to be generated, which could manifest in various ways— be it healing, enlightenment, or spiritual travel.

Synergy of Energies

Creating a collective Merkaba involves more than simply gathering a group of people to meditate or visualize together.

The key lies in the synchronization of individual Merkabas in a manner akin to the harmony of musical notes in a chord. Each person's Merkaba, represented by interlocking tetrahedrons, should theoretically align in geometry, intention, and vibrational frequency with those of the others in the group. This process demands a level of skill and mutual understanding that often takes substantial practice to attain. Some practitioners suggest that when such synchronization happens, the collective Merkaba becomes greater than the sum of its individual parts.

Applications and Limitations

Various applications have been proposed for a collective Merkaba, ranging from group healing sessions to the collective pursuit of higher states of consciousness. There are even suggestions that such a collective energy field could influence environmental or social change, although these ideas largely remain speculative and highly debated. On the flip side, creating a collective Merkaba could also come with its limitations and risks. Incorrect alignment, differences in individual intentions, or varying skill levels in Merkaba practices could result in an unstable collective energy field. Therefore, it is advisable for participants to be well-versed in individual Merkaba meditations and visualizations before attempting to create a collective Merkaba.

Ethical Considerations

As with any spiritual practice that involves more than one individual, ethical considerations must be taken into account. Consent, mutual respect, and shared objectives are imperative when forming a collective Merkaba. Given the intimate level of energetic and conscious interaction involved, participants should be cautious of potential power dynamics or imbalances that might arise. In this context, the principles of empathy, respect, and mutual understanding are not merely aspirational but essential for the practice's ethical integrity.

Documented Instances and Testimonies

While scientific studies on the collective Merkaba are limited, numerous anecdotal accounts and testimonials suggest that people have successfully engaged in such practices. These often come from spiritual retreats or specific gatherings aimed at global healing or consciousness-raising. Although the empirical validity of these experiences is hard to substantiate, they add an interesting layer to the ever-expanding tapestry of Merkaba practices and beliefs.

In summary, the concept of a collective Merkaba offers an intriguing avenue for those looking to extend their Merkaba practices into the realm of collective spirituality. It embodies the harmonization of individual energies and intentions for purposes that range from spiritual enlightenment to altruistic ambitions. However, it is a practice that requires mutual understanding, ethical integrity, and a significant level of expertise in individual Merkaba meditations. As such, it represents not just the potential amplification of spiritual energy, but also a complex field of interpersonal dynamics and ethical considerations.

CHAPTER 23: NAVIGATING REALMS

In previous chapters, we've delved into the intricacies of the Merkaba—its geometry, historical significance, and place in diverse spiritual traditions. We've also discussed the role it plays in meditative practices and its manifestation as an energetic field around the human body. One aspect we haven't yet explored is the Merkaba's alleged capacity to help individuals navigate through different spiritual realms or dimensions. This chapter will attempt to shed light on this esoteric but fascinating feature of the Merkaba, often considered an advanced aspect of Merkaba practices.

The Concept of Spiritual Realms

Many spiritual traditions propose the existence of multiple realms or dimensions beyond the physical world we inhabit. These could range from heavenly to hellish realms, from levels of pure consciousness to those populated by various celestial or spiritual beings. The Merkaba is said to function as a "vehicle" capable of transporting an individual's consciousness through these various planes.

It's crucial to note that such ideas have their roots in ancient scriptures, mythologies, and spiritual philosophies rather than contemporary scientific understanding. That said, even modern theoretical physics toys with the notion of multiple dimensions beyond the three of space and one of time that we experience directly. However, any scientific discussion about additional dimensions is, at this point, largely theoretical and highly mathematical, not readily lending itself to spiritual interpretation.

The Role of the Merkaba in Navigating Realms

The Merkaba is described as a "chariot of light," a multidimensional geometric shape composed of two interlocking tetrahedrons. Through specific visualization and meditation techniques, practitioners claim that this geometric form can become activated, surrounding the individual in a field of energy. This energy field is believed to facilitate the transition from one realm to another, acting as a protective shield and a navigator.

Several ancient texts and modern testimonials discuss experiences of astral travel or out-of-body experiences where the Merkaba plays a critical role. Individuals report sensations of transcending their physical bodies, encountering spiritual entities, and gaining wisdom or insights that were previously unattainable.

Practices and Techniques

Those who claim expertise in using the Merkaba for navigating realms often point to the importance of advanced visualization and deep meditative states. It's not merely about "seeing" the Merkaba around oneself but about achieving a heightened state of consciousness that allows one to "sync up" with the Merkaba's energy. Techniques such as the 17-Breath Technique, discussed in a previous chapter, are sometimes recommended as preparatory practices.

In addition, it's emphasized that ethical considerations, as discussed in another chapter, remain paramount. Misuse or misdirection while attempting to navigate other realms can lead to spiritual or psychological consequences. As such, it is advised to approach this aspect of the Merkaba with a great deal of respect, caution, and ideally, under the guidance of a knowledgeable teacher.

Skepticism and Caution

As fascinating as the concept may be, the idea that the Merkaba enables navigation through different realms is one that invites skepticism. Firstly, experiences of other realms are highly subjective and cannot be verified or disproven by current scientific methods. Secondly, there is a risk of psychological disorientation or even trauma if one is not properly prepared or guided through the experience. Therefore, it's crucial to undertake these advanced practices with due caution and ideally, under the guidance of a knowledgeable and ethical instructor.

In summary, the notion that the Merkaba can be used to navigate different spiritual realms is both intriguing and contentious. Rooted in ancient spiritual traditions and reflected in various testimonies, the concept has also sparked curiosity against the backdrop of modern theoretical physics. While the practice involves advanced visualization and meditative techniques, it is not without its risks and ethical considerations. As such, like all things Merkaba, venturing into the realms beyond requires a balanced approach of both wonder and caution.

CHAPTER 24: MERKABA AND DREAMS

In the fascinating exploration of Merkaba, the concept's intersections with various aspects of human experience cannot be ignored. One of the most intriguing yet often overlooked aspects is the relationship between Merkaba practices and the realm of dreams. Is it possible that our nightly forays into the unconscious world have more to do with this ancient form of spiritual geometry than we might initially think? Let's delve into this intricate connection.

The Significance of Dreams in Spiritual Traditions

In many spiritual traditions, dreams are considered windows into the subconscious mind or even alternate realities. In Hindu philosophy, for example, dreams are thought to reflect the state of one's karma and subconscious desires. Similarly, Jungian psychology posits that dreams are messages from the unconscious, aimed at resolving internal conflicts. In indigenous cultures around the world, dreamtime serves as a powerful space for spiritual teachings and ancestral communication. While these perspectives are diverse, a common thread running through them is that dreams serve as a channel for self-discovery, spiritual guidance, and even healing.

Merkaba and Astral Projection

As we've discussed in previous chapters, one of the metaphysical aspects of the Merkaba is its role in facilitating astral projection or out-of-body experiences. These experiences are frequently described as profoundly spiritual, offering insights that are not accessible through our usual sensory perceptions. It is interesting to note that many tales of astral projection have remarkable similarities to lucid dreaming. Lucid dreaming is a type of dreaming in which the individual having the dream is aware that they are dreaming and has some control over the environment in which they are dreaming. Could it be that the Merkaba acts as a vehicle not just for waking spiritual journeys but also for navigating the dream world?

The Geometry of Dreamscapes

The concept of sacred geometry, central to understanding the Merkaba, may also offer some insight into the structure of dreams. If we entertain the notion that the dream realm is not a chaotic soup of random thoughts but an organized, geometrically structured space, it becomes feasible to assume that the Merkaba, a geometric figure, has a role to play in it. After all, the Merkaba is often referred to as the "geometry of the soul," and what are dreams if not a tapestry woven by the soul?

Dreamwork and Merkaba Visualization Techniques

In many Merkaba practices, visualization techniques are employed to activate or engage with this light chariot. These techniques are strikingly similar to dreamwork methods used in psychotherapy and spiritual practices, such as "dream re-entry," where one consciously re-enters a dream to engage with its content actively. In a sense, mastering Merkaba visualization techniques could equip you with the tools needed for advanced dreamwork, enhancing your ability to decode the messages that your unconscious mind is attempting to communicate.

Therapeutic Implications

While there is limited empirical evidence to substantiate claims regarding Merkaba's role in dream therapy, anecdotal reports suggest a potential for therapeutic benefits. Individuals practicing Merkaba meditation have often reported clearer, more vivid dreams that seem to offer deeper insights into their emotional or psychological states. This enhanced dream clarity could potentially aid in therapeutic settings where dream analysis forms part of the treatment approach.

In summary, the relationship between Merkaba and dreams is an area ripe for exploration, both experientially and academically. The commonalities between Merkaba practices and dream phenomena suggest intriguing possibilities, such as a geometric structure to dreams or a role for the Merkaba in navigating the dream realm. While these connections require further study and validation, they nonetheless offer a captivating addition to our understanding of the complex and multi-dimensional nature of Merkaba.

CHAPTER 25: MERKABA IN POPULAR CULTURE

The Merkaba, a term imbued with historical and spiritual richness, has not confined itself to the pages of sacred texts or the practices of ascetic communities. In fact, it has found its way into popular culture—television, movies, books, and even graphic novels. The power of popular culture to shape public perceptions and stir curiosity cannot be understated, and it has certainly played a role in introducing the Merkaba to a broader audience. In this chapter, we'll take a closer look at how the concept of Merkaba has been represented in these various forms of media, how these representations vary from traditional understandings, and what impact this has on the broader engagement with the concept.

The Silver Screen: Merkaba in Movies

The world of cinema offers a fertile ground for the interplay of ideas, mythologies, and symbolisms. While mainstream films rarely depict the Merkaba in a way that adheres to its historical or spiritual connotations strictly, some independent and speculative films have attempted to showcase it with a degree of accuracy. Often portrayed as an artifact or a mystical shape with auras emanating from it, the Merkaba has been used to signify a wide range of ideas—from portals to other dimensions to powerful talismans with magical properties. However, these representations, while entertaining, often forgo the complexity and depth of the Merkaba in favor of cinematic spectacle.

Literary Depictions: Books and Graphic Novels

The world of literature also offers a versatile platform for exploring complex ideas like the Merkaba. Spiritual thrillers and speculative fiction, in particular, seem to gravitate towards it. Authors use the Merkaba as a narrative device, sometimes linking it to quests for enlightenment or as a McGuffin that propels the story forward. Graphic novels, with their blend of imagery and text, present the Merkaba in a visually striking manner, often elaborating on its geometric aspects. Although these works may not always be faithful to the scholarly or spiritual interpretations of the Merkaba, they do serve to pique interest and prompt individuals to delve deeper into its actual significance.

Television and Streaming Services

In an age where streaming services are becoming the norm, serialized storytelling offers another venue for the Merkaba to make its appearance. Whether in the backdrop of an archaeological adventure series or as a focus in documentaries dealing with metaphysics and spirituality, the Merkaba has been spotlighted to varying degrees of accuracy. While these portrayals can be critiqued for their superficial handling of the subject, they nonetheless contribute to its popularization.

Music and Lyrics

Musicians, especially those in genres that focus on spiritual and metaphysical themes, have not been shy to incorporate the concept of the Merkaba into their work. Lyrics often allude to the Merkaba as a source of cosmic energy or as a metaphor for transcendence. Album covers may even depict the iconic star tetrahedron, embodying the Merkaba, as a means to convey a sense of the esoteric. While the commercial music industry may not offer a deep dive into the Merkaba, it does serve as a starting point for many to explore the concept further.

Popular Culture's Double-Edged Sword

While the portrayal of the Merkaba in popular culture can serve to popularize and demystify the concept, it is not without its drawbacks. Such portrayals can sometimes mislead or oversimplify, causing misunderstandings or diluting the profound spiritual and historical nuances associated with it. Additionally, commercialization can often lead to a commodification of the Merkaba, reducing it to a mere aesthetic or brand. However, these are not insurmountable problems. The key is to approach these portrayals as what they most often are —springboards to deeper understanding, rather than definitive sources.

The presence of the Merkaba in popular culture is both a testament to its enduring fascination and a call for more authentic and informed discussions. As with many other spiritual or historical concepts that find their way into the mainstream, the challenge lies in balancing accessibility with depth, spectacle with substance. While the Merkaba continues to capture imaginations across various media, those who are truly intrigued would do well to delve into its more profound dimensions, transcending the oftentimes simplistic portrayals found in popular culture.

CHAPTER 26: DEBUNKING MYTHS

The concept of Merkaba is rich in history, meaning, and spiritual significance, which makes it ripe for misinterpretations and myths. Misinformation not only affects individual practices but also shapes public perception about this ancient concept. This chapter aims to address and debunk some of the most common myths and misunderstandings about the Merkaba to provide a clearer understanding of what it truly represents.

Merkaba is Solely a Jewish Concept

One prevalent misconception is that Merkaba mysticism is confined to Jewish Kabbalistic tradition. While it's true that the term "Merkaba" does have roots in Hebrew and plays a significant role in Kabbalah, the concept itself is far more expansive. It has been found in various forms in ancient Egyptian, Christian, and Islamic mystic traditions, as well as in certain Eastern philosophies. The geometric shapes and principles underpinning the Merkaba also belong to universal sacred geometry, thereby transcending any single religious or cultural framework.

The Merkaba is Just a Geometric Shape

Another myth is that the Merkaba is nothing more than a combination of geometric shapes. While the tetrahedron-based structure is indeed the fundamental geometric representation of the Merkaba, it is crucial to remember that this is a symbolic representation of much deeper spiritual and metaphysical concepts. According to various traditions, the geometric shape serves as a "light chariot" for the soul, involved in astral travel and enlightenment. The geometry is not an end in itself but a means to facilitate these deeper experiences.

Merkaba Practice is Risk-Free

While Merkaba practices often focus on spiritual elevation and self-improvement, it is incorrect to assume that they are entirely risk-free. Like any spiritual or meditative practice, Merkaba requires proper instruction and awareness. Incorrect techniques or misguided intentions can lead to mental and emotional imbalance. It's important to approach Merkaba meditation and other related practices with caution and ideally under the guidance of a knowledgeable instructor.

Science Cannot Explain Merkaba

Though Merkaba is deeply rooted in spiritual traditions, it's a myth that science cannot touch upon its aspects. Concepts of sacred geometry have found echoes in various scientific fields, including physics and biology. Researchers are beginning to explore how the geometry of Merkaba could have implications in quantum physics and the study of energy fields around the human body. While it is true that science hasn't fully explained the Merkaba, that does not mean it is inherently unscientific or that it will forever elude scientific understanding.

Merkaba is Only for the 'Spiritually Elite'

The perception that Merkaba practices are reserved for spiritual masters or those deeply entrenched in mystical study is a significant barrier to its broader acceptance and understanding. While the practices associated with the Merkaba are complex and require dedicated learning, they are accessible to anyone willing to invest time and sincere effort. Various resources, including books, courses, and guided meditation sessions, are available for people at different stages of their spiritual journey.

Summary

The Merkaba, a concept steeped in ancient wisdom and diverse traditions, is often misunderstood due to various myths and misconceptions. It's essential to debunk these myths to appreciate the full scope and depth of what the Merkaba represents, from its historical roots to its metaphysical implications. Understanding the truths that lie behind these misconceptions will enrich your experience with the Merkaba mysticism and strengthen your connection to this intriguing idea, regardless of whether you are just starting out or have a lot of experience with it.

CHAPTER 27: MERKABA AND ASTROLOGY

Astrology and Spiritual Symbolism

In our quest to understand Merkaba, a geometric pattern believed to be a vehicle for spiritual ascension, we have explored its connections to geometry, history, spiritual practices, and even scientific theories. Now let's turn our gaze skyward to consider how the Merkaba is linked to astrology, the ancient practice of deriving meaning from the celestial dance of planets, stars, and other heavenly bodies.

Astrology has been a significant part of human civilization, dating back to Mesopotamian cultures. Its influence stretches through various cultures and spiritual traditions, including Hinduism, Taoism, and Western Esotericism, among others. Astrology posits that celestial events like the positions of the sun, moon, and planets can influence human life and natural occurrences. While skeptics may question astrology's empirical basis, its symbolic language is deeply interwoven with the spiritual and metaphysical concepts we've discussed in previous chapters, such as the Kabbalah, Eastern philosophies, and sacred geometry.

Planetary Aspects and the Merkaba

In astrology, the planetary aspects—angles that planets make to each other in the sky as observed from Earth—have symbolic meanings. These angles, or aspects, are often described in terms of geometric shapes: trines, squares, sextiles, and oppositions, to name a few. Interestingly, the geometry of the Merkaba—specifically its dual, interlocking tetrahedrons—has a curious resemblance to some of these geometric planetary aspects.

For instance, when we think about the trine, a favorable aspect in astrology often associated with the triangle, it is tempting to consider how the Merkaba's inherent geometry of interlocking triangles might symbolize spiritual harmony or alignment. While this is a speculative connection, it opens up new avenues for integrating the wisdom of astrology with Merkaba practices.

Astrological Houses and Spiritual Dimensions

Astrology divides the celestial sphere into twelve "houses," each governing specific areas of life, from personal identity to relationships and career. This division can be likened to the different spiritual dimensions or realms we discussed in the context of Merkaba in Chapter 23. In both systems, the understanding is that specific energies or vibrations are most effective or influential within certain domains. This alignment of celestial houses with spiritual dimensions offers an alternative lens for understanding how to navigate spiritual realms using the Merkaba.

Astrological Signs and Individual Experience

Zodiac signs form the cornerstone of astrology, representing twelve different archetypes that contribute to human diversity. Each zodiac sign is ruled by a planet, which, in astrological terms, governs certain traits and tendencies of that sign. One could speculate whether individuals might experience Merkaba differently depending on their astrological makeup. For example, a person with a predominance of Earth signs in their birth chart might feel more grounded or focused during Merkaba meditation, while someone with strong Water elements could experience enhanced intuition or emotional depth.

Although these ideas have not been scientifically verified, they provide food for thought. By applying astrological understanding to Merkaba practices, individuals might find additional layers of personal meaning or unique ways to engage with this ancient geometric form.

Celestial Timing and Merkaba Activation

In astrology, timing is crucial. Astrologers often choose auspicious times to undertake significant actions based on planetary alignments. Could there be specific celestial conditions favorable for activating the Merkaba? Some practitioners propose that periods when the Earth and other planets form particular geometric aspects could serve as powerful windows for Merkaba meditation or activation. However, these suggestions remain within the realm of speculative thought and personal experience rather than empirical evidence.

Summary

The interconnectedness of celestial patterns and Merkaba adds a captivating layer to our understanding of this complex and ancient form. Though the empirical evidence supporting the interaction between astrology and Merkaba is limited, the symbolic and speculative connections between the two offer intriguing avenues for further exploration and practice. Just as astrology seeks to elucidate the intricacies of human life through the study of celestial bodies, so too does Merkaba invite us to contemplate the greater cosmos as we journey toward spiritual enlightenment.

CHAPTER 28: PLANETARY MERKABAS

The concept of the Merkaba has been largely discussed in terms of individual spiritual experience. However, what if this intricate geometric form isn't just a tool for personal enlightenment, but exists at larger scales that might impact entire planets, including Earth? In this chapter, we delve into the fascinating idea of Planetary Merkabas and consider the implications it holds for our home planet and perhaps even for the universe.

The Macroscopic View

When we discuss the Merkaba in the context of planets, we're elevating the conversation from individual spirituality to cosmic spirituality. The idea is that just as individual Merkabas encapsulate human souls and can be activated through spiritual practices, a planet too has a soul, so to speak, and can have an active Merkaba field surrounding it. This planetary Merkaba might be thought of as the composite of the energies and consciousness of all the living beings it hosts.

Some spiritual traditions propose that our Earth has an aura, also known as the noosphere, which is influenced by the collective consciousness of all its inhabitants. These traditions suggest that the Merkaba could be activated at a planetary level to elevate this collective consciousness, potentially allowing the planet to ascend to higher vibrational states.

Scientific Inquiries

The notion of planetary Merkabas isn't just a fanciful spiritual idea; it's a topic that intrigues some scientists as well. Researchers in the field of geomagnetism and planetary science study the magnetic fields that envelop planets, including Earth. While mainstream science has not directly addressed the concept of planetary Merkabas, it does affirm that Earth's magnetic field plays a crucial role in sustaining life by shielding the planet from harmful solar radiation. Could this magnetic field be related to a sort of "planetary Merkaba"? That remains a subject of speculation and future research.

Ecological Implications

If one entertains the notion of a planetary Merkaba, interesting questions arise concerning ecology and environmentalism. Could an awakened collective consciousness, through a globally activated Merkaba, bring about positive change in the planet's ecosystem? Some proponents argue that a planetary Merkaba could harmonize the Earth's energies, potentially reversing or mitigating ecological disasters. Though these ideas are far from proven, they offer intriguing possibilities for holistic approaches to planetary well-being.

Spiritual Resonance Across Planets

Exploring this notion further, one could consider the interaction between Merkabas of different planets. Could there be a sort of spiritual resonance or interconnectedness among different planetary bodies? Just as individuals claim to experience heightened spiritual states and insights through their personal Merkabas, could planets too be interconnected through a complex web of cosmic Merkabas? Such a spiritual network could be viewed as a form of cosmic harmony, where the spiritual health of one planet could influence another.

Ethical and Philosophical Questions

The concept of planetary Merkabas also raises ethical questions. If we as a species possess the potential to activate or influence Earth's Merkaba, what responsibilities do we have? How do we ensure that such activation, if possible, is conducted ethically and equitably? Furthermore, if we extend the concept of a soul to a planet, do we not then have a moral obligation to treat that planet with the same dignity and respect that we accord to sentient beings?

In summary, the concept of planetary Merkabas pushes the boundaries of how we traditionally think about the Merkaba. By elevating the scale from individual to planetary—and potentially beyond—we are invited to broaden our understanding of spirituality, science, and ethics. While much of this territory is speculative, it offers a wealth of exciting possibilities for further study, philosophical inquiry, and even spiritual exploration.

CHAPTER 29: TEACHING AND LEARNING THE MERKABA

The process of teaching and learning the Merkaba is a subject of immense importance. This chapter delves into the intricacies of the teacher-student dynamic, the importance of correct pedagogy, and the pivotal role of empathy in imparting the profound wisdom associated with Merkaba techniques and practices.

Teacher-Student Dynamic in Spiritual Practices

In the realm of spiritual practices like Merkaba meditation, the teacher-student relationship holds a unique and sacred space. This dynamic is not merely an exchange of information but is more akin to a transfer of wisdom and insight. Unlike academic teachings, the intricacies of Merkaba practices often transcend what can be articulated through language alone. Teachers, therefore, serve as guides who help students navigate the complex emotional, spiritual, and even physical elements involved in mastering Merkaba techniques. They don't just instruct; they inspire and shape the spiritual journey of the learner.

Pedagogical Approaches

Traditional pedagogical methods may not always be suited for teaching the complex, multi-dimensional aspects of the Merkaba. Teachers often employ a holistic approach, melding theory with practice, and rational thought with intuitive understanding. Various techniques are commonly used:

Oral Transmission: Oral teachings and stories have been a long-standing method in many spiritual traditions. This method allows for the subtleties and nuances of the practice to be communicated directly.

Hands-On Practice: The Merkaba is often best understood by direct, experiential learning. This means engaging in visualization, breathing exercises, and even physical manifestations like creating Merkaba models.

Discussion and Reflection: One-on-one conversations or group discussions can provide invaluable insights, helping to clarify doubts and deepen understanding. These forums allow students to ask questions that might not have straightforward answers, fostering a dynamic learning environment.

The Importance of Correct Guidance

Given the spiritual depth and esoteric nature of Merkaba practices, incorrect teachings can be not only ineffective but also potentially harmful. This brings us to the crucial role of qualified, experienced teachers. An unqualified teacher might lead a student astray, potentially causing spiritual or psychological harm. Therefore, ensuring the credentials and integrity of the teacher becomes paramount. The best way to verify this usually involves personal testimonials, demonstrated expertise, and an observable commitment to the ethical and spiritual dimensions of the practice.

Adaptability and Individualized Learning

Every individual's spiritual journey is unique, and Merkaba practices are no exception. A good teacher recognizes this individuality and adapts their teaching methods accordingly. For some, understanding the Merkaba might come easier through the lens of sacred geometry and mathematical precision. Others might relate more to its spiritual or metaphysical aspects. An effective teacher taps into these personal inclinations and provides a learning path tailored to the student's unique disposition.

Empathy and Sensitivity in Teaching

When teaching something as intricate and deeply personal as Merkaba, empathy and sensitivity are not just beneficial; they are essential. A teacher's ability to sense a student's emotional and spiritual state can make a world of difference. It allows for the teaching to be paced appropriately, ensuring that the student doesn't feel overwhelmed. This kind of empathetic teaching can make the learning process deeply transformational, rather than merely informational.

Summary

The journey to understanding and mastering the Merkaba is as personal as it is profound. The role of a teacher in this voyage is indispensable, serving as both a guide and a fellow traveler on the path to spiritual enlightenment. The teacher-student dynamic in Merkaba practices is enriched through proper pedagogical approaches, a focus on correct guidance, the adaptability of teaching methods, and the necessity of empathy and sensitivity.

All of these elements contribute to a holistic learning experience, preparing the student to explore the multidimensional complexities of the Merkaba.

CHAPTER 30: ETHICAL CONSIDERATIONS

Ethical considerations are often relegated to the back burner in discussions surrounding mystical and spiritual practices. However, they are essential in understanding the implications and responsibilities that come with engaging in activities tied to profound spiritual meanings and practices like the Merkaba. Let's delve into the complexities of ethics in Merkaba practices, from respecting traditions to ensuring personal well-being and integrity in community engagements.

Respecting Cultural Traditions

The concept of Merkaba spans various cultures and spiritual traditions. As such, it's vital to approach these practices with cultural sensitivity. Borrowing or co-opting Merkaba techniques and teachings without due acknowledgment can be seen as a form of cultural appropriation. One must not only credit the origins but also respect the values and beliefs that accompany these practices. For example, if you are practicing Merkaba within the framework of Kabbalah, it's crucial to respect the historical and religious significance the tradition holds within Judaism.

Personal Well-being and Safety

Engaging in spiritual practices like Merkaba meditation can lead to powerful psychological experiences. It's essential to approach these practices with caution, especially if you're a beginner or have a history of mental health issues. A qualified instructor should always guide these practices, and you should never push yourself beyond your psychological or emotional limits. Mental preparedness and awareness are key to safely experiencing Merkaba's potential benefits.

Community Responsibility

As a practitioner of Merkaba, you may find yourself within a community that shares your interests and beliefs. While collective energy can be a strong motivator, it's vital to uphold ethical standards when engaging with others. For instance, if you're leading a Merkaba meditation session, clearly outline the potential risks and benefits to participants. Transparency and open dialogue foster trust and ethical integrity within the community.

Commercialization and Integrity

In an era where spiritual practices are increasingly commercialized, ethical issues related to monetizing spiritual wisdom are becoming more prevalent. If you're offering Merkaba courses, workshops, or even books, it's crucial to avoid exaggeration or false claims regarding the benefits or outcomes. Misrepresentation not only tarnishes the spiritual integrity of Merkaba but also poses ethical dilemmas. People may be investing time, money, and emotional resources based on the promises made, so maintaining honesty is essential.

Ethical Approaches to Teaching and Learning

The role of the teacher and student in Merkaba practice

is a nuanced relationship that requires ethical consideration. Teachers should never abuse their positions of authority or influence, especially in spiritual practices where students might be emotionally vulnerable. Similarly, students should approach learning with an open but critical mindset, without blindly accepting all that is taught. Both parties share the responsibility for ensuring ethical standards are upheld.

In summary, the realm of Merkaba practices is rich in spiritual, cultural, and emotional depth. However, this depth must be navigated responsibly, respecting the ethical considerations that come with engaging in such practices. Whether it's respecting cultural traditions, ensuring personal well-being, or maintaining integrity in commercial and communal engagements, ethical considerations should never be an afterthought. By upholding these principles, one can truly engage with the practice of Merkaba in a meaningful and respectful manner.

CHAPTER 31: BEYOND THE FIFTH DIMENSION

As we've journeyed through the labyrinthine world of the Merkaba, we've touched upon its many facets—from its ancient origins to its placement within various spiritual traditions and even its intersections with modern science. Now, let's push the envelope a little further by exploring one of the most intriguing aspects of Merkaba: the concept that it can be a vehicle for multi-dimensional travel. In this chapter, we'll dive into the esoteric idea that the Merkaba might provide a means to move beyond our standard three dimensions of space and one of time, and venture into realms that are currently beyond our empirical understanding.

The Concept of Multiple Dimensions

Before we explore the role of the Merkaba in multi-dimensional travel, let's first clarify what is meant by "dimensions." In the language of physics, a dimension is a direction in which it's possible to move. In our everyday world, we're familiar with three dimensions of space: length, width, and height, along with one dimension of time. However, various theories in physics, particularly String Theory, suggest that there could be more than these four dimensions—perhaps as many as 11 or more. These additional dimensions are not currently accessible to us but are considered to be "compactified" or "curled up" so tightly that they're almost impossible to detect.

Merkaba and Fifth-Dimensional Consciousness

Within the framework of Merkaba mysticism, practitioners often speak of ascending to a "fifth-dimensional consciousness." This phrase doesn't necessarily align with the scientific understanding of dimensions but is more of a metaphysical concept. The idea is that through Merkaba practices, one can raise their vibrational frequency to access a higher level of consciousness and awareness. This state is often described as being one of unconditional love, spiritual enlightenment, and a sense of universal connectedness. While it is not a dimension in the scientific sense, this elevated state of being is often referred to as the "fifth dimension" in esoteric literature.

The Multi-Dimensional Chariot

So, where does the Merkaba fit into all this? In mystical traditions, the Merkaba is sometimes viewed as a "light chariot" that can transport the soul through different dimensions or planes of existence. Through advanced visualization techniques, breathing practices, and meditative states, it's said that an individual can activate their Merkaba, thereby unlocking its potential as a vehicle for inter-dimensional travel. This is often discussed in the context of astral travel, where the astral body separates from the physical body and can explore other realms.

Scientific Skepticism and Open Questions

It's important to approach the idea of Merkaba as a vehicle for multi-dimensional travel with a degree of skepticism. As of my last update in September 2021, there's no empirical evidence to support the notion that humans can physically or even astrally travel through different dimensions. While String Theory and other areas of theoretical physics speculate about the existence of additional dimensions, these are far from being proven or universally accepted within the scientific community.

That said, the absence of evidence is not necessarily evidence of absence. The Merkaba's role in multi-dimensional travel remains an open question, ripe for further exploration both in scientific and spiritual domains. The experiences of those who claim to have used the Merkaba for such extraordinary journeys offer tantalizing anecdotes, but they are not proof in the empirical sense.

Balancing Skepticism and Possibility

While we should be cautious about accepting unverified claims, the notion that the Merkaba could serve as a multi-dimensional vehicle should not be entirely dismissed. Many aspects of quantum physics were once considered to be the stuff of science fiction until they were empirically verified. As our scientific understanding evolves, so too does the realm of what is considered possible.

The human quest for understanding our universe and our place within it is far from complete. Whether or not the Merkaba can truly serve as a vehicle for multi-dimensional travel, its role as a symbol for higher states of consciousness and spiritual ascension is undeniable. It reminds us that there are aspects of our existence that are yet to be understood, beckoning us to continue our exploration into the realms of both the empirically provable and the spiritually conceivable.

In summary, the Merkaba's potential role as a vehicle for multi-dimensional travel straddles the boundary between scientific skepticism and spiritual possibility. While empirical evidence for such extraordinary capabilities is lacking, the notion captivates our imagination and invites us to explore further. Whether considered a metaphor for higher states of consciousness or a literal vehicle for journeying through hidden dimensions, the Merkaba remains an enduring and evocative symbol of humanity's quest for understanding and transcendence.

CHAPTER 32: FUTURE OF MERKABA PRACTICES

As we find ourselves at the intersection of ancient wisdom and modern understanding, the concept of Merkaba has never been more relevant. In a world where scientific advancements and global spirituality are evolving at an unprecedented pace, it's worth considering how Merkaba practices will fit into the future tapestry of human experience. In this chapter, we will speculate on the prospects of Merkaba in the realms of scientific research, technological advancements, and the global spiritual landscape.

Scientific Research and Merkaba

While much of the fascination with Merkaba revolves around its ancient origins and spiritual significance, there is a growing interest in examining this concept through the lens of modern science. Quantum physics, neuroscience, and even the field of artificial intelligence may offer potential frameworks for understanding the Merkaba in a new light. For instance, quantum entanglement theories could eventually explain the mysterious connections between Merkaba energy and distant cosmic phenomena. Additionally, as research into the human brain and consciousness deepens, we may find neurological underpinnings that support Merkaba meditative practices.

Technology and Virtual Realities

The advent of immersive technologies like virtual reality (VR) and augmented reality (AR) presents an intriguing avenue for the future of Merkaba practices. Imagine a VR environment designed to aid in the visualization and manifestation of your personal Merkaba, enhanced by real-time biofeedback to optimize your meditative state. Such technologies could revolutionize the way we engage with Merkaba, making it more accessible and providing a more immediate and sensory-rich experience. While technology should not replace traditional practices, it could serve as a complementary tool that enriches the learning and experiential process.

Merkaba in Global Spirituality

In an era marked by a resurgence of interest in spirituality—often divorced from traditional religious frameworks—Merkaba stands to gain renewed attention. The universal aspects of its geometry and the wide-ranging spiritual traditions that reference it make Merkaba a truly global concept. As awareness about the significance of sustainable living and interconnectedness grows, practices that promote holistic well-being will likely gain more traction. Merkaba, with its focus on spiritual, emotional, and even physical alignment, fits well into this paradigm.

Ethical and Societal Implications

As Merkaba practices evolve, it's essential to consider the ethical dimensions. For one, as the practice goes mainstream, there is a risk of commodification and dilution of its core principles. Authenticity and respect for its sacred origins must be maintained. Secondly, as scientific research progresses, ethical guidelines will be crucial for any experiments that aim to measure or manipulate Merkaba energy, to ensure the dignity and well-being of participants.

Merkaba Education and Mentorship

The future of Merkaba also depends on the way it's taught and transmitted to newer generations. As online platforms make knowledge more accessible, it becomes increasingly important to establish standardized guidelines and accreditation for Merkaba educators. A balanced approach that combines the wisdom of ancient traditions with the rigor of scientific inquiry could provide a more holistic and credible form of education.

In summary, the future of Merkaba practices seems poised for a dynamic evolution influenced by advancements in science, technology, and a shifting global consciousness. While its ancient roots will always be a crucial aspect of its identity, the Merkaba has the potential to grow and adapt, becoming ever more relevant in our modern world. From its likely intersections with emerging scientific theories to its applications in cutting-edge technology, Merkaba practices may unfold in ways that our ancestors could have scarcely imagined, yet would perhaps deeply appreciate. As we move forward, maintaining a balance between respect for ancient wisdom and openness to new understandings will be key in nurturing the growth and broader acceptance of Merkaba practices.

CHAPTER 33: RESOURCE GUIDE

The journey of understanding and experiencing the Merkaba is both expansive and intricate. The more you know, the more you realize there is yet to discover. For those who wish to delve deeper into this multifaceted subject, a myriad of resources are available that can provide further insights and knowledge. This chapter aims to guide you through a curated list of books, academic articles, websites, and other media that can be instrumental in your journey.

Recommended Books

"The Ancient Secret of the Flower of Life" by Drunvalo Melchizedek

A seminal work that introduces the geometry of the Merkaba and the Flower of Life, along with various other aspects of sacred geometry. It's considered one of the go-to texts for those looking to delve deeper into this subject.

"The Key to the True Kabbalah" by Franz Bardon

This book offers a detailed exploration of the Kabbalistic tradition, including its symbology and practices, some of which touch upon the Merkaba.

"Journey of Souls: Case Studies of Life Between Lives" by Michael

Newton

While not directly about the Merkaba, this book delves into the metaphysical and spiritual dimensions that could be accessible through Merkaba meditations.

Academic Articles

"Sacred Geometry and Its Mathematical Principles"

An academic paper that covers the mathematical aspects of sacred geometry, including those of the Merkaba. Available through several scholarly databases.

"Mysticism and Science: An Analytical Study"

This article explores the intersection between spiritual experiences and scientific rationality, offering perspectives that could extend to the Merkaba.

Websites and Online Resources

Sacred Geometry International

An online platform that focuses on sacred geometry, featuring articles, courses, and tools that can help deepen your understanding of the Merkaba.

The Kabbalah Centre

Provides courses, articles, and webinars that cover the teachings of Kabbalah, including the Merkaba as understood in the Kabbalistic tradition.

Podcasts and Audio Resources

"The Sacred Geometry Podcast"

A series that discusses various elements of sacred geometry, including the Merkaba. Available on most podcast platforms.

"Astral Projection Radio Hour"

Although not specifically focused on the Merkaba, this podcast often touches on subjects like astral travel and multidimensional realms that could be related to Merkaba practices.

Multimedia Resources

Virtual Reality Merkaba Meditation Apps

As discussed in earlier chapters, these apps offer an immersive experience to visualize and interact with the Merkaba in a virtual setting.

YouTube Channels Dedicated to Sacred Geometry

Various channels offer guided meditations, tutorials, and educational videos on the Merkaba and related topics.

Note of Caution

While the internet is a vast resource, it's important to approach any information with discernment. Many websites claim to offer "quick fixes" or "immediate enlightenment" through the Merkaba, but such assertions should be viewed with caution. Consult multiple sources and, where possible, refer to academic articles or established spiritual authorities for the most reliable information.

Summary

In this resource guide, we have covered an assortment of

materials that range from books and scholarly articles to websites and multimedia options. Each of these resources offers a unique perspective and depth of knowledge on the Merkaba, aiding you in your journey through this complex subject. Whether you're drawn to the academic, spiritual, or experiential facets of the Merkaba, there's something here to cater to your quest for understanding. Choose the resources that resonate with you, and may they serve as valuable companions in your ongoing exploration.

CHAPTER 34: GLOSSARY

As we've navigated the multi-faceted world of Merkaba, we've come across numerous terms that may be new or complex to some readers. While the individual chapters have strived to clarify these terms in context, having a glossary can offer a quick reference or refresher for the key concepts discussed. Here we will define and explain essential terms to facilitate a deeper understanding of the topics explored in the book.

Merkaba

Merkaba is an ancient term, often linked to sacred geometry and various spiritual traditions. It's conceptualized as a three-dimensional, interlocking pair of tetrahedra. The term is generally used to refer to a "light-spirit-body" that is believed to serve as a vehicle for astral or spiritual travel and enlightenment.

Sacred Geometry

Sacred geometry refers to a form of geometry that is used to understand and interpret the divine order and spiritual significance of shapes and proportions in the natural world. In the context of Merkaba, sacred geometry helps to understand the structure and implications of its tetrahedral shape.

Kabbalah

Kabbalah is a form of Jewish mysticism that aims to understand the nature of God and the universe. In Kabbalah, Merkaba holds a particular significance, often related to the Tree of Life, a symbolic map of the cosmos and the soul's journey.

Astral Travel

Astral travel, or astral projection, is the notion that the 'astral body' can leave the physical body and traverse different dimensions or realms. Merkaba is often associated with facilitating such experiences.

Tetrahedron

A tetrahedron is a polyhedron with four triangular faces. In the context of Merkaba, two interlocking tetrahedra form the geometric basis for the light chariot.

Chakras

In Eastern philosophies like Hinduism and Buddhism, chakras refer to energy centers within the body. Although not identical in concept to Merkaba, both share the overarching theme of energy manipulation and spiritual growth.

Visualization Techniques

These are a set of meditative practices aimed at forming mental images to aid in relaxation, healing, or spiritual experiences. In Merkaba meditation, visualization of the light chariot is considered crucial.

Enlightenment

In spiritual contexts, enlightenment refers to an elevated state of consciousness, often characterized by peace, wisdom, and the cessation of suffering. Merkaba practices are believed to facilitate or contribute to reaching this state.

Metaphysics

Metaphysics is a branch of philosophy that deals with the fundamental nature of reality, covering topics like existence, knowledge, and the nature of being. Merkaba is often discussed in terms of its metaphysical implications, particularly when dealing with topics like astral travel and enlightenment.

Quantum Physics

This subfield of physics investigates the ways in which matter and energy behave at the atomic and subatomic levels of organization. Some modern interpretations of Merkaba attempt to understand it through the lens of quantum theory, particularly when discussing its energetic and multi-dimensional aspects.

Ethical Considerations

These are the moral implications associated with practicing Merkaba or any other spiritual practice, including issues related to cultural appropriation, potential misuse, and ensuring that practices are done responsibly and respectfully.

Collective Merkaba

This term refers to the idea that a group of individuals can collectively form a more potent Merkaba energy field, amplifying the effects and experiences associated with it.

Multi-dimensional Travel

In esoteric spirituality, multi-dimensional travel refers to the idea that one can traverse or experience realms beyond the three-dimensional world we perceive. The concept is often brought up in discussions about the more speculative capabilities of Merkaba.

In summary, this glossary serves as a convenient reference point for readers, summarizing the essential terminology explored throughout this book. By understanding these key terms, you will enrich your comprehension of the intriguing and multidimensional world of Merkaba.

CHAPTER 35: FREQUENTLY ASKED QUESTIONS

By now, you've traversed the intricate landscape of Merkaba mysticism, its geometry, spiritual significance, scientific interpretations, and much more. Given the complexity and multifaceted nature of the subject, it's understandable that questions may linger. This chapter aims to address some of the most frequently asked questions about the Merkaba. These inquiries are collated from various sources, including practitioners, novices, skeptics, and those simply curious about this fascinating topic.

What is the Merkaba?

The Merkaba is a geometric shape, usually visualized as two interlocking tetrahedra, that is said to represent the energy field around the human body. It is associated with ancient wisdom, spirituality, and various esoteric practices, notably in Kabbalistic traditions and Eastern philosophies. Some believe the Merkaba is a vehicle for spiritual ascension and inter-dimensional travel, although these ideas often dwell in the realm of personal experience and interpretation.

Is the Merkaba a Religious Concept?

While the Merkaba is deeply rooted in religious and spiritual traditions like Kabbalah and even ancient Egyptian cosmology, it is not limited to any one faith or doctrine. People from diverse spiritual backgrounds, and even those who don't identify with a particular religion, explore and incorporate Merkaba practices in their lives.

Can Anyone Practice Merkaba Meditation?

Anyone who is prepared to devote the necessary amount of time and effort to mastering the Merkaba meditation practices can generally do so. However, it is advisable to approach them with due respect for their origins and underlying philosophies. If you're new to meditation or spiritual practices, consulting a knowledgeable guide or teacher can provide invaluable insights and help avoid common pitfalls.

Is There Scientific Evidence Supporting Merkaba?

The scientific community generally regards Merkaba and similar esoteric concepts with skepticism due to the lack of empirical evidence. However, the intersection of quantum physics and spirituality has opened doors for potential exploration. While some scientists are investigating phenomena that could relate to the Merkaba, as of now, it remains largely a subject of metaphysical and spiritual discussion.

What is the Significance of the 17-Breath Technique?

The 17-breath technique is a foundational practice in Merkaba meditation. It is a series of breathing patterns and visualizations aimed at activating your Merkaba field. Many practitioners consider it a pivotal exercise for engaging with the Merkaba effectively. However, mastering it usually requires dedicated practice and, often, guidance from an experienced teacher.

How Does Merkaba Relate to Healing?

In some spiritual circles, the Merkaba is believed to be a vehicle for channeling healing energy. While anecdotal evidence and personal testimonials abound, rigorous scientific studies in this area are scant. Some individuals integrate Merkaba meditation into broader holistic health practices, although this should not replace professional medical advice or treatment.

Are There Risks Associated with Merkaba Practices?

Like any potent spiritual practice, Merkaba techniques come with their own set of risks, especially when pursued without proper understanding or guidance. Incorrect practices can reportedly lead to mental and emotional imbalance. It is advisable to approach Merkaba practices with due caution and, ideally, under the supervision of a knowledgeable guide.

Can Merkaba Help in Astral Projection?

Astral projection is another topic often mentioned in conjunction with the Merkaba. While some practitioners claim that mastering Merkaba techniques aided them in achieving out-of-body experiences, such accounts are highly subjective. There's no widespread consensus on this, and experiences vary significantly among individuals.

How Does Technology Influence Merkaba Practices?

With advancements in technology like virtual reality, new

avenues for experiencing and visualizing the Merkaba are emerging. While these methods offer innovative ways to engage with the concept, they are not replacements for traditional practices but rather supplements that can enhance understanding and visualization.

In summary, the topic of the Merkaba often raises more questions than it answers, given its complex and esoteric nature. While this chapter addresses some common questions, the quest for understanding is ever-evolving. As you deepen your exploration, new questions will likely arise, each leading you further into the intriguing maze that is the Merkaba.

CHAPTER 36: CONCLUSION AND FINAL THOUGHTS

As we draw to the close of this comprehensive journey through the multifaceted world of the Merkaba, it's fitting to pause and reflect on the magnitude and richness of the concepts we've explored. This book has been a deep dive into an ancient, mystifying subject that touches on geometry, spirituality, history, and even modern science. It has spanned cultural contexts from Mesopotamia and ancient Egypt to Kabbalistic traditions and Eastern philosophies. While the Merkaba remains enveloped in mystery, what is clear is that it has the potential to impact various aspects of human life—physiological, psychological, and spiritual.

Merging the Ancient and the Modern

One of the most compelling aspects of Merkaba is its capacity to bridge time. Rooted in ancient traditions and teachings, it also finds a place in contemporary discussions about metaphysics, quantum physics, and spirituality. The geometric structures inherent to the Merkaba aren't merely ancient symbols; they can be interpreted through the lens of modern science. Thus, the Merkaba serves as a metaphorical crossroads where ancient wisdom meets contemporary inquiry.

Spirituality and Science

The Merkaba also represents an intersection between spirituality and science, two realms often considered mutually exclusive. Through this complex geometric figure and its associated practices, we've seen that there can indeed be an interplay between the metaphysical and the empirical. For instance, the geometry involved in the Merkaba isn't just an abstract concept but has mathematical underpinnings that can be scrutinized scientifically. Moreover, as we have explored in the chapters on quantum physics, there are elements of Merkaba that invite scientific exploration, even if definitive conclusions remain elusive.

Ethical and Collective Consciousness

The book has not shied away from the ethical implications and responsibilities associated with the practice of Merkaba. This is a potent and influential construct, and its misuse or misunderstanding can lead to unintended consequences. The idea of a collective Merkaba, a shared experience of this spiritual concept, adds another layer of ethical considerations. How we approach the Merkaba, not just as individuals but as a community, can have broader implications for collective well-being and spiritual evolution.

Future Directions

While the Merkaba has ancient roots, its journey is far from over. New technologies like virtual reality are already being used to facilitate Merkaba experiences, offering fresh avenues for exploration. Similarly, as our scientific understanding evolves, new theories could provide further insights into the Merkaba's intricacies. There is still much terrain to cover, questions to answer, and practices to refine. As is often the case with any profound concept, the more you know, the more you realize how much there is still to discover.

Final Reflections

The allure of the Merkaba is as enduring as it is enigmatic. Whether you approached this book as a skeptic, a believer, or someone simply curious about the interplay of geometry and spirituality, it's evident that the Merkaba offers a vast, complex field ripe for exploration. This book has aimed to be a guide, illuminating various facets of the Merkaba from multiple angles—historical, spiritual, scientific, and ethical. Yet, it is clear that the Merkaba's mystery still holds untapped potential, inviting each of us to engage with it in our unique ways.

As we part ways, may your journey with the Merkaba be enlightening, ever-evolving, and imbued with the kind of deep wonder that enlivens the human spirit. Thank you for sharing this quest for understanding, and may you find the light chariot to be a source of endless inspiration and insight.

THE END

Printed in Great Britain
by Amazon